CAMBRIDGE

PREPARE

WORKBOOK WITH DIGITAL PACK

T0384696

B2

LEVEL 7

David McKeegan **Second Edition**

Cambridge University Press
www.cambridge.org/elt

Cambridge Assessment English
www.cambridgeenglish.org

Information on this title: www.cambridge.org/9781009032483

First published 2015
Second Edition 2020
Second Edition update 2021

20 19 18 17 16 15 14 13

Printed in Dubai by Oriental Press

A catalogue record for this publication is available from the British Library

ISBN 978-1-00-903248-3 Workbook with Digital Pack
ISBN 978-1-00-903247-6 Student's Book with eBook
ISBN 978-1-00-903249-0 Teacher's Book with Digital Pack

CONTENTS

1 CREATIVE MINDS

VOCABULARY Arts and media

1 Match the words to the meanings.

1 shoot
2 piece
3 appearance
4 broadcast
5 cast
6 track
7 charts
8 bestseller
9 series
10 classic
11 stream

a a set of books published by the same company which deal with the same subject
b use a camera to record a film or take a photo
c a recording of a song or a piece of music
d when someone appears in public, on television, in a film, etc.
e send out a programme on television, radio or the internet
f an official list of the most popular songs each week
g all the actors in a film, play or show
h a very popular book that many people have bought
i an example of artistic, written or classical work
j listen to or watch sound or video directly from the internet, rather than downloading and saving it first
k a piece of writing, music or a film which has been popular for a long time and is considered to be of high quality

2 Choose the correct words.

1 Most of this film was *shot / broadcast* in the Arizona desert.
2 The band released the first *cast / track* on their new album as a single, and it immediately made it into the *charts / piece*.
3 Have you seen this artist's latest *shot / piece*?
4 The whole *cast / series* of the new film made a surprise *appearance / charts* at our local cinema.
5 Her novel is a *bestseller / cast* now, and I'm sure it will be the first in a long *series / shot*.
6 On what channel do they *broadcast / shoot* the awards ceremony?
7 The book I have just read is a *classic / piece* – my mum read it when she was a child.
8 The internet connection is slow so you may not be able to *broadcast / stream* the film.

READING

 PREPARE FOR THE EXAM

Reading and Use of English Part 7

1 You are going to read five reviews of fantasy novels. Before you read, underline the main idea in each question.

Which book
1 does the reviewer consider too frightening for young readers?
2 is about regaining something that has been lost?
3 does the reviewer find funny?
4 involves a journey into the past?
5 features a character who may be hiding something?
6 is being turned into a film?
7 has a main character who is not very sociable?
8 is one of a series of novels?
9 takes some ideas from another work?
10 includes a character interested in magic and fun?

2 For questions 1–10, choose from the reviews (A–E). The reviews may be chosen more than once.

 EXAM TIPS

- Always read the questions first and underline the main ideas in them.
- Read all the texts quickly for general meaning.
- Scan the texts for information that matches the ideas you have underlined in 1–10.
- If you find it easier, concentrate on one text at a time and answer the questions that relate to it.

3 Read the questions again and underline the parts of the reviews which give you the answers.

4 Match the highlighted words in the reviews to the meanings.

1 reminds one of something
2 very exciting
3 not violent, severe or strong
4 very beautiful or surprising
5 using information or knowledge of something to help you do something

A

A Stitch in Time
by Penelope Lively

Maria is always lost in her own little world in which she prefers to chat with animals, trees, plants and inanimate objects, rather than other human beings. But while on holiday, she begins to hear things that others can't, and she's not sure what is real any more. Then she finds a nineteenth-century sewn picture and she feels a strange connection with Harriet, the girl who sewed it. As Maria becomes more involved in Harriet's world, she begins to fear that something sad has happened. This book is a gentle, mysterious and occasionally laugh-out-loud read from an author who started her career writing film scripts.

B

The Girl Who Fell Beneath Fairyland and Led the Revels There
by Catherynne M. Valente

This is the second of six breathtaking adventures featuring September, the strange girl who returns to Fairyland to find that the fairy creatures are in trouble. For a while now, they have been losing their shadows and, with their shadow, their magic is disappearing. September learns that it is all to do with a conflict with Fairyland-Below, a dark place where there is no law, and terrifying creatures live. It is a place that September knows she has to visit in order to get back the shadows from the thieves, and to sort out the mess that Fairyland is in. It takes her on an incredible journey that is sometimes dangerous, sometimes terrifying, but always fascinating. Readers young and old will have great fun with this one.

C

Shadow Spell
by Caro King

When Nina is set the task of stopping the evil Mr Strood from killing the dying land of Drift, she has to find Simeon Dark, the last surviving magician king, and his mansion, for he is the only one who can make sure she is successful. But with Dark's love of playing tricks, and strange creatures and monsters – good and bad – in the way, Nina has a hard mission before her. Readers watch the heroine survive a series of thrilling adventures, and fall in love along the way. The book is written for the teen market, but there is nothing unsuitable for younger readers in here. In fact, the movie rights have already been sold to a family-friendly Hollywood production company, and it is due for release next year.

D

Ante's Inferno
by Griselda Heppel

Adults will have heard of Dante's *Inferno*, and the author says she was inspired to write her book by drawing on the *Inferno*'s riches. Ante and her enemy at school, Florence, plus a boy who has been trapped in the music room for a hundred years, fall into a tunnel leading to the Underworld. There they find themselves in a dark and nightmarish place, where characters from Greek mythology exist alongside terrifying, monstrous beings. Their horrifying journey and need to get back to the real world is full of exciting events. While it may be a bit much for pre-teens to deal with, more mature readers will keep turning the pages to find out what dreadful thing is going to happen next.

E

The Deadly Trap
by Jan Burchett & Sara Vogler

Young hero Sam is taken back 300 years onto his favourite pirate ship, the *Sea Wolf*, where the pirates are planning to steal some English gold. Within minutes he meets the new shipmate, Dick, who Sam suspects is not all he claims to be. The other pirates all like him, but Sam is not so sure, and sets a trap that Dick falls into. The others refuse to believe Sam and go ahead with their piracy plans involving Dick. Sam and his close friend Charlie have to find a way to stop Dick's plan. This is a fast-moving tale, which brings to mind the old-fashioned adventure stories of such classic writers as Stevenson and Defoe.

Simple, continuous or perfect

1 **Choose the correct form of the verbs.**

1 **A:** How many films *did you see / have you seen* since the festival started?
B: Three. I *saw / 've seen* the best one yesterday.

2 **A:** We *go / 're going* on holiday to Spain every year.
B: I *never went / 've never been* to Spain.

3 **A:** Hi Tim. What *do you do / are you doing* at the moment?
B: I *do / 'm doing* my English homework.
A: Oh. I *did / 've done* mine yesterday.

4 **A:** *Did you enjoy / Were you enjoying* the concert last night?
B: No, we were too late. When we arrived, the show *finished / had finished*. Nobody *was / has been* there!

5 **A:** What *did you do / were you doing* when I called you last night?
B: I *read / was reading* my favourite writer's new novel. I *read / 'm reading* it now too.
A: Oh, *do you enjoy / are you enjoying* it?
B: Yes, I *love / am loving* her work.

2 **Complete the email with the correct form of the verbs in brackets.**

Hi Emily

I ¹ _____ (write) this email from a café in Edinburgh. The sun ² _____ (shine), and it's a beautiful day.

Every year we ³ _____ (come) to the arts festival here. It ⁴ _____ (be) an annual treat for us since 2010, when we ⁵ _____ (move) to Scotland. We usually ⁶ _____ (stay) for a week, and go to see as many shows as we can. Last year we ⁷ _____ (see) twelve! One evening last year when we ⁸ _____ (walk) back to our hotel, a group of people dressed as monkeys ⁹ _____ (run) into the road and ¹⁰ _____ (start) dancing. It was a very funny sight, but strange things like that often ¹¹ _____ (happen) during the festival.

Another unusual thing ¹² _____ (happen) last night when we ¹³ _____ (sit) in the hotel restaurant. We ¹⁴ _____ (just / pay) the bill and we ¹⁵ _____ (get) ready to leave, when a journalist with a film crew ¹⁶ _____ (come) in and ¹⁷ _____ (start) interviewing people. My brother made us all leave quickly because he ¹⁸ _____ (not want) to be on TV!

Anyway, my friends ¹⁹ _____ (just / come) into the café, and they ²⁰ _____ (want) me to go and see a film with them. Write soon!

Donna

3 **Correct the mistakes in the sentences or put a tick (✓) by any you think are correct.**

1 I had taken so long to write to you because I have been busy. _____

2 Did you had a good time on your holiday? _____

3 She has been my best friend since last summer. _____

4 By the time I arrived, he has disappeared. _____

5 Surfing is my hobby since 2010. _____

6 We're having a great time here in London. _____

VOCABULARY **Creative jobs**

1 **Who is speaking? Use the words in the box.**

comedian	critic	editor	novelist
producer	programmer		TV presenter

1 'My last book was a bestseller, which they are going to turn into a film.'

2 'Sometimes people don't like the opinions I express in my reviews.'

3 'I'm the person who is in control of the whole show.'

4 'If there are any mistakes in the writing, I will find them and correct them.'

5 'The app I am creating now is sure to be very popular!'

6 'Sometimes I get nervous before I have to introduce the show, but I relax as soon as it starts.'

7 'The thing I fear most is an audience that doesn't laugh at any of my jokes.'

>> See *Prepare to write* box, Student's Book page 13.

1 Your teacher has asked you to write an essay for homework. Make notes below about points 1 to 3.

> 'Young people today want to be rich and famous as a result of watching reality TV and talent shows, but they should have more realistic ambitions.'
> **Do you agree?**
>
> **Notes**
> Write about:
> **1** why reality TV and talent shows are popular
> **2** how they affect young people
> **3** _____ (your own idea)

1 _____

2 _____

3 _____

2 Here are the first two paragraphs of the essay. Do they contain any of your ideas? Read them and check. (Ignore the gaps.)

Reality TV and talent shows are not exactly educational. ¹_____, they are not intended to be. They are just for entertainment, and ²_____ that they are very entertaining. This is why they are so popular – people just want to forget about their problems and relax in front of the TV!

Nevertheless, some people say they are a bad influence. ³_____, many teachers have noted that their students have unrealistic ideas about their future. They just want to be rich and famous. ⁴_____, some young people do not care about their schoolwork because they believe you don't need qualifications to be a pop star!

3 Complete the text with the expressions in the box.

> for instance   furthermore   however
> most people agree

4 Complete the plan with notes from the box below. For 2, use the text in Exercise 2.

1 Introduction
not educational
_____

2 Paragraph 2 – effects on young people
_____

3 Paragraph 3 – another angle
_____

4 Conclusion – sum up the points
_____

> another idea of your own
> ~~not educational~~
> stop caring about schoolwork
> summary of the points made
> unrealistic ideas about the future
> relaxing
> harmless fun
> your conclusion

✓ PREPARE FOR THE EXAM

Writing Part 1

5 Now complete the essay, using the plan and all your notes from Exercise 4, and give reasons for your point of view. Try to use the following expressions in your paragraphs: *to sum up*, *in contrast*. Write about 140–190 words.

✓ EXAM TIPS

- Make a plan for your essay before you write it.
- Give each paragraph a clear function – for example, an introduction with your opinion, ideas for the statement in the question, ideas against the statement and a conclusion.
- Be sure to address both prompts in the question and introduce your own idea.
- Use linking words to join your ideas.

2 ADDICTED TO FASHION

Personality: adjective + preposition

1 Complete the table with the correct adjectives.

addicted	adventurous	aware	~~bothered~~	cautious	critical
decisive	hopeless	impressed	jealous	loyal	mean

about	at	by	of	to	with
bothered					

2 Choose the correct options to complete the sentences.

1 I'm _____ to playing computer games.
   A addicted   **B** loyal   **C** adventurous
2 I'll organise the show, because Tara is _____ at making arrangements.
   A impressed   **B** decisive   **C** hopeless
3 Dan thought he had written a good essay, but the teacher was very _____ of it.
   A aware   **B** critical   **C** jealous
4 She wears expensive clothes, but I'm not _____ by that.
   A impressed   **B** mean   **C** adventurous
5 Don't be _____ about your brother's new haircut – he's embarrassed enough!
   A jealous   **B** mean   **C** loyal
6 Are you _____ of the risks involved in this plan?
   A aware   **B** jealous   **C** critical
7 I'm very _____ about spending a lot of money on the latest fashions.
   A addicted   **B** adventurous   **C** cautious
8 He's very _____ to a particular brand of clothes – he never wears anything else.
   A critical   **B** loyal   **C** adventurous

3 Read about these young people's attitudes to fashion. Complete the sentence about each one with a phrase from the box.

addicted to	adventurous with
bothered about	decisive about
jealous of	

1 Meral always buys a new pair of shoes when she has any spare money – she can't stop buying shoes!
   Meral is _____ buying shoes.
2 Andrea doesn't care what's in fashion.
   Andrea isn't _____ fashion.
3 Max is happy to try every new fashion idea that comes along.
   Max is _____ fashion.
4 Anna really doesn't like it when her best friend buys all the new fashions.
   Anna is _____ her best friend.
5 When he's shopping for clothes, Peter always makes his mind up very quickly.
   Peter is _____ clothes.

READING

1 Look at the photo on page 9. Why do you think sunglasses are always in fashion?

✓ PREPARE FOR THE EXAM

Reading and Use of English Part 1

2 Read the first two paragraphs of the article. Decide which answer (A, B, C or D) best fits each gap.

	A	B	C	D
0	put	(B) came	opened	presented
1	likely	sure	proper	hopeful
2	approved	favourite	welcome	popular
3	regarded	treated	considered	weighed
4	matter	kind	subject	reality
5	told	reported	explained	described
6	avoid	prevent	protect	reduce
7	normal	usual	general	regular
8	deeply	widely	highly	largely

Can you think of an item which has never been out of fashion, ever since the time it **(0)** _came_ on the market? You might think denim jeans are a **(1)** .... candidate. But, while they have always been **(2)** ...., there have also been times when they were **(3)** .... to be unfashionable by expert 'fashion watchers'. As a **(4)** .... of fact, the only fashion item that has always been cool to wear since the start of the twentieth century is a pair of sunglasses, or 'shades'.

So where did these remarkable things come from? Back in 60 CE, the Roman emperor Nero was **(5)** .... to have enjoyed watching fighting in the Colosseum through clear green stones to **(6)** .... his eyes from strong sunlight. Such luxuries were unaffordable for the **(7)** .... public, of course. It wasn't until nearly two thousand years later that coloured glasses became cheap enough to be **(8)** .... available.

One of the things that led them to become such desirable fashion items was their popularity with American film stars in the early 1900s. It is commonly believed that this was to avoid being recognised by fans. However, an alternative explanation is that in those days film actors often had red eyes because of the high-powered lamps that were used in film studios, and they didn't want the public to see them. Whatever the reason, when businessman Sam Foster began selling inexpensive, mass-produced sunglasses in 1929, he found a ready market.

Nowadays sunglasses are big business, with hundreds of different brands to choose from. In fact, the industry generates 34 billion dollars per year in sales. Celebrities continue to be unpaid promoters of the products. Singer Elton JoÚ, for example, is thought to have a sunglasses collection of over 1,000 pairs. Sunglasses have even played minor roles in films. In the 1999 sci-fi thriller *The Matrix*, starring Keanu Reeves, all the good characters wore round shades, and the bad guys all wore rectangular ones.

But what is the real reason for their continuing popularity? Is it simply the fact that the general public has a strong desire to copy the rich and famous? The truth of the matter is, people wear them for various reasons: comfort and clear vision bright sunlight, protection from the dangerous rays of the sun, to avoid eye contact with others, or even to hide their emotions. All of these are reasonable excuses for putting on dark shades. But it is generally recognised that the main reason is much simpler: they look cool!

3 Read the whole article quickly. Choose the best title (A–C).

  A The item that's never out of fashion
  B Why celebrities wear sunglasses
  C How to make money in the fashion business

4 Read the article again and choose the correct options.

  1 Sunglasses became popular in the *first / twentieth / twenty-first* century.
  2 The public didn't buy many sunglasses at first because they were *too expensive / poorly designed / not very effective*.
  3 The writer thinks film stars wore sunglasses in order to *show they were famous / protect their eyes from lights / hide their eyes*.
  4 The writer thinks that celebrities *wear sunglasses too much / get paid to wear sunglasses / encourage the public to wear sunglasses*.
  5 Sunglasses remain popular because they *provide protection / look good / are cheap*.

5 Match the highlighted words in the article to the meanings.

  1 very unusual or noticeable ....
  2 worth having and wanted by most people ....
  3 creates ....
  4 prevent something from happening ....
  5 made in large quantities, usually in a factory ....

Present perfect simple and continuous

1 **Choose the correct verb forms.**

1 It's time you changed your shirt. You've *worn / been wearing* it for three days!
2 I've *lost / been losing* my new sunglasses.
3 Her skin is red because she's *sunbathed / been sunbathing* without sunscreen.
4 How long have you *studied / been studying* fashion?
5 We've *sold / been selling* six of these dresses today.
6 I've *read / been reading* his latest book, but I'm not enjoying it.
7 You haven't *eaten / been eating* much of your lunch today.
8 They've *drunk / been drinking* coffee since they got up this morning.

2 **Complete the email with the present perfect simple or continuous form of the verbs in brackets.**

●●● ◄ ►   🔍 🏠

Hi Tom

How are you? I hope you ¹ ....
(keep) busy at college! We're having a great time here. The weather ² .... (be) fantastic so far!

I ³ .... (sit) on the beach all morning, watching the world go by. I ⁴ .... (already/have) a few ideas for new swimming costume designs for next term's fashion project!

Laura and I ⁵ .... (meet) some interesting people who are staying in the same hotel as us. They ⁶ .... (be) here for a couple of weeks already, and they ⁷ .... (do) research for a project about beach fashions. Yes, they work in fashion too, just like us. In fact, they ⁸ .... (apply) for jobs for the last few months without any luck, but they think that presenting a full design project will help. What a good idea!

Anyway, Laura ⁹ .... (try) to attract my attention for the past five minutes, so I'd better see what she wants! I think she wants to go for lunch – we ¹⁰ .... (not eat) since breakfast.

Bye for now,

Sally

3 **Correct the mistakes in the sentences or put a tick (✓) by any you think are correct.**

1 The football team has been playing badly last year.
   ....
2 I have been doing gymnastics for more than ten years. ....
3 Agustina is my best friend since we met in school when we were three years old. ....
4 I am playing classical guitar for three years.
   ....
5 Yesterday I have been hiking for five hours.
   ....
6 I have known Marion for ten years now.
   ....

Verb + preposition

1 **Complete the email with the prepositions in the box.**

at	for	of	on	with (x2)	without

●●● ◄ ►   🔍 🏠

Hi Jane

I'm writing a quick note to apologise ¹ .... laughing ² .... your hat yesterday at school. The truth is, it was a really nice hat compared ³ .... mine. I suppose I was jealous of you! Sometimes I just can't cope ⁴ .... people having nicer things than me. It's very childish, I know.

I need to get a summer job, because I hate depending ⁵ .... my parents to give me money to buy things, and I really don't like to do ⁶ .... new clothes!

I'm going shopping later. Have you heard ⁷ .... Coco's? It's a new clothes shop in town. Do you want to come with me?

Dani

1 Do you like shopping for clothes? Write down one or two good things and bad things about it.

2 You will hear five short extracts in which teenagers are talking about shopping for clothes. Do they mention any of the things on your list in Exercise 1?

✔ PREPARE FOR THE EXAM

Listening Part 3

3 Listen again. For speakers 1–5, choose from the list (A–H) what each speaker says about shopping for clothes. Use the letters only once. There are three extra letters which you do not need to use.

A I enjoy making independent decisions.
B I'd rather do something less boring.
C I am different from my friends.
D I want to get a job in fashion.
E I often buy nothing when I go shopping.
F I love the social element of shopping.
G I try to be as stylish as possible.
H I have very little money to spend.

Speaker 1 ....
Speaker 2 ....
Speaker 3 ....
Speaker 4 ....
Speaker 5 ....

4 Listen again and complete these phrases from the extracts. Which two express a negative attitude?

1 I don't particularly .... for clothes.
2 I'm really .... fashion.
3 We always .... to the new collection.
4 It's quite a .... for me.
5 What's not .... ?
6 Honestly, I don't know what people ....

5 Read the questions about shopping and write your answers. Use phrases from Exercise 4 if you can.

1 Do you enjoy going shopping for clothes?

2 What do/don't you enjoy about it?

3 Who do you go shopping with?

4 When do you go shopping?

5 What kind of things do you usually buy?

✔ EXAM TIPS

- Read all the options before you listen.
- Try to think of other ways that the ideas might be expressed, as the speakers will use different words from the ones in the options.
- Remember that you will hear the recording twice.

ADDICTED TO FASHION 11

3 ALL IN THE MIND

Abstract nouns

1 Match the nouns to the meanings.

1 agreement	_____	**6** problem-solving	_____
2 belief	_____	**7** ambition	_____
3 development	_____	**8** success	_____
4 drive	_____	**9** thought	_____
5 luck	_____		

a when you achieve what you want to achieve
b something that you think is true
c a strong wish to be successful
d the good (and bad) things that happen to you
e the activity of thinking
f energy and determination to achieve things
g the process of changing into something new
h the process of finding solutions
i when people have the same opinion or make the same decision

2 Choose the correct abstract noun to complete the sentences.

1 It is my _____ that one day we will discover life on other planets.
  A success   **B** luck   **C** belief

2 Education should encourage _____ as well as give students knowledge.
  A problem-solving **B** belief **C** agreement

3 Ian's recent novel was a big _____ – millions of copies were sold.
  A drive   **B** success   **C** luck

4 It was pure _____ that I met Simon in town – we hadn't arranged to meet.
  A nurture   **B** drive   **C** luck

5 The school is spending a lot of time on the _____ of a new homework marking system.
  A problem-solving **B** development **C** thought

6 Jack is very talented, but he lacks the _____ to succeed as an actor.
  A problem-solving **B** thought **C** ambition

7 I don't think you have the _____ to be a big success in the business world.
  A drive   **B** thought   **C** development

8 I haven't given much _____ to what I'm going to do with my time this summer.
  A luck   **B** thought   **C** belief

READING

1 Look at the photo in the article. What are the animals doing, and why are they doing it?

_____

_____

2 Now read the article quickly. What kinds of animals are mentioned as showing similar emotions to humans?

_____

 PREPARE FOR THE EXAM

Reading and Use of English Part 6

3 You are going to read an article about empathy. Six sentences have been removed from the article. There is one extra sentence. Underline the pronouns and determiners which refer to something outside the sentence.

  A It seemed to be willing to go hungry rather than see a fellow animal suffer.

  B Empathy plays a role in that, as it allows us to understand our fellow humans better.

  C This fear of strangers will, we believe, protect us from personal danger.

  D Other research has shown animals displaying empathy towards other animals and towards humans.

  E The usual effect of this kind of behaviour is that it stops crying, shouting and other signs of being upset.

  F We assume that people are able to think themselves into the position of another person, even though they may not have personally experienced that person's circumstances.

  G They communicate this requirement by crying for attention and to show pain.

4 Choose from the sentences A–G the one which fits each gap (1–6). There is one extra sentence which you do not need to use.

 EXAM TIPS

- Read the text quickly for its general meaning.
- Read the sentences A–G carefully and underline important words.
- Also underline pronouns and other possible links between the sentences and the text.
- Look for links in the sentences before and after each gap in the text.

THE ORIGINS OF EMPATHY

Empathy – the ability to imagine what it must be like in someone else's situation – was traditionally thought to be a quality only possessed by human beings. It is an essential part of what it means to be human, to the extent that we are suspicious of anyone who does not show empathy in their behaviour.

Empathy should not be confused with sympathy – caring about another person's problems – which does not necessarily mean that we understand how we would feel in the same situation. To feel empathy is more involved than simply feeling sorry for someone else's troubles. **1** This is not restricted to real life – we read novels, watch television and go to the theatre, and part of our enjoyment comes from understanding the dilemma faced by the characters, because we know how we would feel if we were in the same situation. Empathy is essential to the smooth running of society. We create rules, without which society could not work, and we obey them because we can empathise with our fellow citizens.

However, it seems that in fact empathy may not be a quality unique to humans. One study involving children's reactions to adults pretending to be upset – for example, crying or expressing pain – observed that family pets seemed to be reacting as well. **2** Creatures from across the animal kingdom such as whales, bees and chimpanzees, as well as domestic pets, display behaviour that suggests they cooperate with and protect each other.

In another study, psychiatrist Jules Masserman and his team conducted an experiment with monkeys in which the monkeys pulled one of two chains that released food. One chain simply released the food, while another gave a small electric shock to a second monkey. The first monkey stopped pulling the chain that delivered the shock. **3** This empathetic behaviour was observed in a number of monkeys.

The origin of empathy is probably the need for the young of all animal species to be cared for. **4** Both human and non-human young were more likely to survive if their parents reacted positively to their needs. People and animals alike are social beings and are more likely to survive if they work together. **5** If we help others, we are also helping ourselves, and so empathy is sensible and practical.

We do not always display empathy, however. Just as animals react aggressively to unknown creatures from their own or other species, so humans tend to regard people they don't know with suspicion. **6** Our unwillingness to trust anyone unfamiliar is as natural to us as our empathy towards those we know and love.

---

5 List the words you underlined in Exercise 3 and what they refer to. (The numbers refer to those in the text.)

1	we	human beings
	they	another person
2		
3		
4		
5		
6		

6 Match the **highlighted** words in the article to the meanings.

1 used after referring to two groups of people or things to show that both groups are included
2 owned or had
3 allowed to drop
4 not known
5 a situation in which a difficult choice has to be made between two different things

1 Complete the table with the phrasal verbs.

break down	care for	deal with
get out of	let down	look forward to
put off	show off	

without an object	
separable	
inseparable	
inseparable three-part	

2 Choose the correct options.

1 Don't pay any attention to Tom. He's just *showing off / showing him off*.
2 It's an important task – you mustn't *put it off / put off it* any longer.
3 I'm sorry to *let down you / let you down* again.
4 Our car *broke down / broke it down* again last week.
5 Who's going to *care for the cat / care the cat for* while you are on holiday?
6 Are you *looking the party forward to / looking forward to the party* tonight?
7 The exam is tomorrow and there is nothing you can do to *get it out of / get out of it*.
8 I really don't have time to *deal with this problem / deal this problem with* at the moment.

3 Put the words in order to make sentences and questions.

1 let / down / you / Have / ever / I / ?

2 can't / pressure / She / with / deal

3 you / down / the TV / Can / turn / ?

4 the mess / up / I'll / in the kitchen / clear

5 Our aunt isn't well. is / Mum / her / for / caring

4 Correct the mistakes in the sentences or put a tick (✓) by any you think are correct.

1 It will show of how healthy the students are.

2 I hope it will be up to your expectations.

3 She looked me after since my childhood.

4 The youngest people sometimes make show in front of their friends.

5 I'm looking forward to hearing from you in the near future.

1 Choose the correct words.

1 It's hard to *focus / get* on your work when you're tired.
2 Sometimes I mix *through / up* the present perfect and past simple tenses.
3 She applied to do the course, but she didn't get *over / in*.
4 Always try to *back / think* through what you're going to include in your essay before you start.
5 You'll just have to face *up to / up with* the fact that you'll never be a professional footballer.
6 It's a good idea to *back / mix* up your work every five minutes or so.

2 Complete the messages with verbs from Exercise 1.

Katy Malik

I'm finding it really hard to ¹_____ on my English homework when my brother is playing his rock music really loud in the next room! I'm never going to be able to study enough to ²_____ into university!

Tom Cohen

Katy, you're just going to have to ³_____ up to the fact that your brother loves rock. Why don't you ask him to ⁴_____ it up a bit and play some rap or reggae, too?

Katy Malik

I don't think that'll help! I don't even know what I'm going to write about yet. Do you?

Tom Cohen

Yes, but I haven't actually written anything yet because I'm still ⁵_____ it through.

Katy Malik

Well, don't forget to ⁶_____ your work up. Remember what happened last time!

>> See *Prepare to write* box, Student's Book page 23.

1 Match the two halves of the informal expressions and write them below.

0	Thanks so much	a	soon.
1	Write	b	is, …
2	The thing	c	I reckon …
3	But don't	d	as I know, …
4	To start	e	care.
5	It's lovely	f	with …
6	As far	g	for your email.
7	Keep	h	in touch.
8	To be honest,	i	happy to …
9	I'm very	j	to hear from you.
10	Take	k	forget that …

0 *g* *Thanks so much for your email.*
1 ....
2 ....
3 ....
4 ....
5 ....
6 ....
7 ....
8 ....
9 ....
10 ....

2 Read the following exam task. How many questions should you answer in your email?

You have received this email from your English friend, Andy.

> Hi,
> I'm doing a project about people's attitudes to pets around the world. Here in Britain, more than 50% of households have a pet, with dogs being the most popular, followed by cats. What do you think about this? Are pets popular in your country? If so, which kind?
> I'd really value your opinion.
> Andy

Write your **email**.

3 Look at these sentences from an email in response to Andy. Which two sentences should not be in the response? Put a cross (✗) by them.

1 People tend not to keep pets in my country, because most people live in flats. ....
2 People in Britain obviously really love animals! ....
3 I think it's cruel to keep animals in zoos. ....
4 If people keep a pet, it's usually a small animal or bird, like a budgie. ....
5 I don't agree that 50% of British households have a pet. ....
6 It's interesting that dogs are the most popular; they need a lot of attention. ....

4 Which questions in Andy's email do the correct sentences from Exercise 3 answer?

5 Make notes to answer the following questions.

1 Do you think 50% is a lot of households to have pets?
   ....

2 What does that say about British people?
   ....

3 Do you have a pet? What do you have?
   ....

4 Do you know anyone with a different pet? What?
   ....

5 What do you think are the advantages of having a pet?
   ....

6 What are the disadvantages of having a pet?
   ....

 PREPARE FOR THE EXAM

Writing Part 2 (An informal letter or email)

6 Write a reply to Andy's email. Use your answers to Exercise 5 and some informal expressions from Exercise 1.

 EXAM TIPS

- Answer all the questions or points in the task.
- When you have written your letter or email, check that you have answered everything.
- Check that you have written between 140 and 190 words.
- Remember to use informal language throughout.

VOCABULARY Stress

1 Complete the puzzle, using the clues to help you.

1 It's hard to concentrate when you're going over and over something in your _____.
2 Tell Lizzy to lie down – she looks like she's going to _____!
3 I need to sit down – I _____ dizzy.
4 No lunch for me, thanks. I've lost my _____.
5 I always get in a _____ the day before a test.
6 I'm so nervous that I've got an _____ stomach.
7 The teacher will _____ her temper if we are late again.

Word down: _____ sleeping

2 Complete the sentences with the correct form of the phrases in Exercise 1.

1 I couldn't sleep last night because I was _____ our argument _____.
2 Jenny has been worrying about her exams so much that she's got an _____.
3 My brother kept changing the TV programme and Mum _____ and shouted at him.
4 You'll _____ if you run round in circles like that!
5 I couldn't find my house key this afternoon and I started to _____.
6 Miss Harrison had to stop the geography class today because one of the students _____ and they had to call a doctor.
7 Dad's back is really bad at the moment and he's having _____ so he feels tired all the time.
8 I usually _____ when I have a cold because I can't taste anything.

3 Complete the sentences so that they are true for you.

1 The last time I lost my temper was when _____
2 I find it hard to get to sleep when I'm going over and over _____ in my mind.
3 Sometimes I get in a panic when _____
4 I lost my appetite when _____.
5 When I have difficulty sleeping, I _____.
6 _____ makes me feel dizzy.

READING

1 Look at the picture of an anechoic chamber on page 17. What do you think it is for? Do you think it is a pleasant or a stressful place to be in?

_____

2 Read the text quickly. Did the writer enjoy his experience in the anechoic chamber?

_____

3 Read the text again and answer the questions.

1 What did the anechoic chamber remind the writer of?
2 Why is the absence of sound upsetting for most people?
3 Why does the chamber have to be completely dark?
4 Why did the writer feel that the chamber wasn't silent at all?
5 What was the main reason for the writer leaving the chamber?

4 Read the sentences. Write A if the information is correct, B if it is incorrect or C if the information isn't given.

1 The writer was unhappy because his family annoyed him.
2 Orfield Laboratories' anechoic chamber is the quietest place in the world.
3 The violinist entered the chamber as part of a training programme.
4 The writer felt confident before he entered the chamber.
5 People were surprised that the writer stayed in the chamber for so long.
6 The writer regularly returns to the chamber at Orfield Laboratories.

The sound of silence

Sometimes all I want is a bit of peace and quiet. When I've got some important homework to finish, and my sister won't stop chatting on her phone; when I'm trying to concentrate on the book I'm reading, and Grandma is watching TV downstairs with the sound on high; or when I just want to catch an extra hour's sleep on a Saturday morning, and it seems that all the noises – both inside the house and outside – are doing their best to keep me awake. Too much noise can drive anyone mad!

So last summer I decided to go on a mission to find the quietest place on Earth. To my surprise, I didn't have to travel far. I live in Minnesota, home of the Orfield Laboratories, and the world's best anechoic chamber.

An anechoic chamber is a small room made up of layers of concrete and steel to remove outside noise, much like a standard sound recording studio in many ways. But in this case, even the floor is suspended to stop any sound of footsteps. According to *Guinness World Records*, it's the quietest place on Earth – 99.9% sound-absorbent. The strange thing is that most people find its perfect quiet upsetting. Not being able to hear the usual sounds can be frightening. Astronauts do part of their training in anechoic chambers at NASA, so they can learn to cope with the silence of space.

The fact that you can hear sounds means that things are working; when sound is absent, that signals something is wrong. One violinist tried spending some time in the chamber, and banged on the door after a few seconds, demanding to be let out because he was so disturbed by the silence.

But I was determined to try it, so I collected all my savings and booked a 45-minute session – even though no one had managed to stay in for that long before. I felt anxious for two reasons: would I go crazy and tear off my clothes? Or would I just be disappointed that it wasn't as different as I'd hoped?

When the heavy door closed behind me, I was surrounded by darkness, as lights can make a noise. For the first few seconds, being in such a quiet place felt really cool. I tried hard to hear something and heard … nothing.

Then, after a minute or two, I began to hear the sound of my breathing – so I held my breath. Then my heartbeat seemed to become really loud. As the minutes passed by, I started to hear the blood rushing in my veins. I frowned and heard the skin move over my head, which was very strange. Then I started to feel a bit disappointed – this place wasn't silent at all.

After a while, I stopped concentrating on the sounds my body was making and began to enjoy it. I didn't feel frightened, and came out only because my time was up; I would happily have spent longer in there. I'd made it – I'd broken the record! Can you imagine how amazed everyone was?

My 45 minutes in the anechoic chamber was a really interesting and important experience for me. It made me appreciate the quiet times I have, but more than that – it made me appreciate everyday sounds. My sister still chats on her phone, and Grandma still has the TV on too loud – but I don't get so annoyed by them any more.

5 Match the **highlighted** words and phrases in the article to the meanings.

1 deal successfully with a difficult situation
2 done something better than anyone else
3 the regular movement or sound that a heart makes
4 upset
5 money which you keep in a bank or similar place

Modals (1): necessity, obligation, prohibition and advice

1 Read the sentences and choose the correct function of the modal verb.

1 We mustn't forget to do our homework.
   A prohibition   B advice   C lack of obligation
2 You should try to get more sleep every night.
   A obligation   B advice   C prohibition
3 They don't have to wear a uniform.
   A necessity   B prohibition   C lack of obligation
4 Do you really need to play your music so loudly?
   A prohibition   B advice   C necessity
5 You had better start soon if you want to finish this project on time.
   A prohibition   B advice   C lack of obligation
6 I must remember to send Elena a thank-you note.
   A obligation   B necessity   C prohibition
7 We have to finish this project by Monday morning.
   A obligation   B advice   C lack of obligation
8 Getting fit needn't be hard work.
   A prohibition   B advice   C lack of obligation

PREPARE FOR THE EXAM

Reading and Use of English Part 4

2 For questions 1–6, complete the second sentence so that it has a similar meaning to the first sentence, using the word given. Do not change the word given. You must use between two and five words, including the word given.

0 Drinking coffee before going to bed is not recommended.   **NOT**
   You _should not drink coffee_ before going to bed.
1 We can stay in bed as late as we want during the holidays.   **HAVE**
   We _____ up early during the holidays.
2 Our teacher advised spending two hours revising every day.   **SHOULD**
   Our teacher _____ two hours revising every day.
3 Next week's museum trip is not compulsory.   **GO**
   You _____ on next week's museum trip if you don't want to.
4 Nobody under the age of eighteen is allowed in this club.   **OVER**
   You _____ be allowed in this club.
5 We need to catch this train, or we'll be late.   **NOT**
   If we don't want to be late, we _____ this train.
6 Cutting down on sugary drinks is a good idea if you want to be healthy.   **OUGHT**
   If you want to be healthy, _____ down on sugary drinks.

 EXAM TIPS

- Read each first sentence carefully and think about its meaning.
- Read your completed second sentence to check that your answer makes sense and has correct grammar.
- Make sure you have not used more than five words.

3 Correct the mistakes in the sentences or put a tick (✓) by any you think are correct.

1 I had to decide what to buy. _____
2 I suppose you will must have fun in New York. _____
3 We can't decide where we should go. _____
4 I've been told to give my opinion about whether students only have to study what they enjoy. _____
5 You only have one life, and you don't have to waste it. _____

VOCABULARY   Phrasal verbs: health

1 Complete the conversation with the correct form of the phrasal verbs in the box.

calm down	come down with
come round	get someone down
get over	throw up

Sara: Steve! Are you OK? What happened? You look terrible!

Steve: ¹_____!
I'm fine! I just had a minor operation yesterday, and I'm still ²_____ it.

Sara: Oh dear. Were you unconscious for the operation?

Steve: Yes, and I felt really sick when I ³_____ afterwards. In fact, I ⁴_____!

Sara: Poor you! You really don't look well.

Steve: Don't worry about me. How are you, anyway?

Sara: I think I'm ⁵_____ a cold actually, which is annoying. Being ill really ⁶_____ me _____.

Steve: Yeah, me too.

LISTENING

 1 You will hear five short extracts in which teenagers are talking about free-time activities. Listen and match speakers 1–5 to photos A–E.

Speaker 1 ....
Speaker 2 ....
Speaker 3 ....
Speaker 4 ....
Speaker 5 ....

2 Now look at the options in Exercise 3. Can you make a note of what each speaker liked most about their activity? If you can't remember, try to guess.

Speaker 1 ....
Speaker 2 ....
Speaker 3 ....
Speaker 4 ....
Speaker 5 ....

✓ PREPARE FOR THE EXAM

Listening Part 3

 3 Listen again. For speakers 1–5, choose from the list (A–H) what each speaker likes best about their activity. Use the letters only once. There are three extra letters which you do not need to use.

A meeting new people
B getting fit
C learning new things
D earning money
E socialising with people
F relaxing for the evening ahead
G experiencing a sense of achievement
H dealing with daily problems

Speaker 1 ....
Speaker 2 ....
Speaker 3 ....
Speaker 4 ....
Speaker 5 ....

✓ EXAM TIPS

- Listen to each speaker in full before trying to answer the question.
- Note your answer in pencil if you aren't sure after you listen the first time.
- Listen to the other speakers before you decide – the answers are often clearer when you listen again.

A

B

C

D

E

VOCABULARY History

1 Put the letters in order to make words.

1 TRENYCU ....
2 THYM ....
3 UNDOF ....
4 DACDEE ....
5 ZITNECI ....
6 THIBANNITA ....
7 ROTANECS ....
8 TEG HET OVET ....
9 BERIT ....

2 Match the words in Exercise 1 to the meanings.

a period of 100 years
b person who has the right to live in a country
c obtain the right to participate in democratic elections
d relative who lived a long time ago
e very old story which is probably not true
f period of 10 years
g a person or animal that lives in a particular place
h a group of people who live together, usually in areas far away from cities and who share the same culture and language, and still have a traditional way of life
i to bring something into existence

3 Complete the sentences with the correct form of the words in Exercise 1.

1 Hercules is a character from a number of Greek and Roman ....
2 The 1990s was the .... which saw the rise of the internet.
3 We are living in the twenty-first ....
4 He applied to become a US ....
5 My .... came from North Africa.
6 Women in Saudia Arabia .... in 2015.
7 This country has around seven million ....
8 The city of London was .... by the Romans in the first century.
9 The Zulus are the largest .... in South Africa.

READING

1 What part of speech is gapped in each of these sentences? Choose from the list below.

1 A circus .... built in Ancient Rome.   *b*
2 I came .... with flu, so I missed the performance.
3 What's the point .... going to the circus?
4 Come with us. I think that you .... enjoy it.
5 Danny enjoyed the show, but I didn't like ....
6 .... Roman Empire fell in the fifth century.
7 A .... of people attended circuses in Egypt.
8 They let us in even .... we were very late.

a modal verb   e conjunction
b verb *be*   f article
c pronoun   g quantifier
d part of a phrasal verb   h preposition

2 Now write the correct word in the gaps in Exercise 1.

3 Read the first three paragraphs of the text about the circus on page 21. Do not try to fill the gaps this time. How many civilisations are mentioned in the text?

....

✓ PREPARE FOR THE EXAM

Reading and Use of English Part 2

4 For questions 1–8, read the first three paragraphs of the text and think of the word which best fits each gap. Use only one word in each gap.

✓ EXAM TIPS

- Read the title to find out what the text is about.
- Read the whole text first before you decide on your answers.
- Look at each gap and decide what type of word is needed – an article, a preposition, a pronoun, a modal verb or something else?

THE CIRCUS: ORIGINS AND HISTORY

The idea (0) ___of___ travelling performers has its origins far back in history. (1) _____ is believed that the Ancient Egyptians had groups of travelling acrobats, and people may have been entertaining each (2) _____ in similar ways even further back in time.

The word *circus* comes from the Ancient Greek and Roman word for 'circle' because acts (3) _____ performed in round arenas. The Ancient Greeks (4) _____ have chariot races, horse shows, staged battles, and displays by jugglers and acrobats in these places. In the ancient city of Rome there was a fixed place where the shows used to take (5) _____. The first one to be built was called the Circus Maximus. This stone stadium could seat as (6) _____ as 200,000 people.

After the fall of the Roman Empire, these large circus stadiums fell (7) _____ of use. Instead, performers travelled between towns in Europe performing at local fairs. Groups of entertainers and acrobats have done this for hundreds of years – and they will probably (8) _____ so for many years to come.

By far the most famous Roman circus building was the Colosseum in Rome, built during the time of the Flavian emperors. Construction of the Colosseum was begun sometime between 70 and 72 CE, during the time of Vespasian. It is located just east of the Palatine Hill, on the grounds of what was Emperor Nero's Golden House.

The water was removed from the artificial lake that was the central feature of that palace, and the Colosseum was built there – a decision that was made for largely political reasons. Vespasian, whose path to power had relatively poor beginnings, chose to replace the unpopular Nero's private lake with a public amphitheatre that could hold tens of thousands of Romans.

The structure was officially opened in 80 CE by Titus, in a ceremony that included 100 days of games. Later, in 82 CE, Domitian completed the work by adding the top storey. Unlike earlier amphitheatres, which were nearly all dug into convenient hillsides for extra support, the Colosseum is an independent structure of stone and concrete, measuring 189 by 156 metres overall.

The amphitheatre seated around 50,000 spectators, who were protected from the sun by a massive cloth roof called a *velarium*. Hundreds of Roman sailors were required to pull the ropes that opened and closed this roof! The Colosseum was the scene of thousands of hand-to-hand fights between gladiators, of contests between men and animals, and of many larger battles.

The Colosseum was damaged by lightning and earthquakes in medieval times and, even more severely, by theft and criminal damage. All the seats and decorative materials disappeared, as the site was treated with very little respect for more than 1,000 years. Work to preserve the Colosseum began properly in the nineteenth century, and a project to restore it was started in the 1990s. It has long been one of Rome's major tourist attractions. Many changing exhibitions relating to the culture of Ancient Rome are now held here.

5 Read the rest of the text and choose the correct answers.

1 Work on the Colosseum was started by the Roman Emperor *Vespasian / Nero / Palatine*.
2 The Colosseum was built for the benefit of the Roman *people / Emperor / environment*.
3 The roof of the Colosseum was operated by *gladiators / spectators / sailors*.
4 Most of the damage to the Colosseum was caused by *natural disasters / war / people*.

6 Match the highlighted words in the text to the meanings.

1 level of a building _____
2 very seriously _____
3 outside events where you can play games and go on rides _____
4 almost completely _____
5 very large _____

GRAMMAR Present and past habits

1 Choose the correct verb forms.

1 When I was younger I *was always / used to* stay in bed until 11.00 on Sunday morning.
2 He *eats / is eating* a lot of meat and fish at the moment because he's training for a match.
3 My sister *is constantly looking / constantly looks* for new shoes.
4 When we were at primary school, we *would go / were going* to bed before nine during the week.
5 I always *feel / am feeling* hungry when I wake up in the morning.
6 Daniel *used to / would* be better-looking than he is now.
7 My brother *was always / would* playing tricks on me when we were young.

2 Complete the sentences with the words in brackets.

0 Stacey arrives late too often, and it annoys you. (always)
   Stacey ___*is always arriving late*___ .
1 When you were a child you rode your tricycle every day. (would)
   When I was a child _____
   _____.
2 The sofa is your temporary bed while your room is being decorated. (sleeping)
   I _____
   while my room is being decorated.
3 Susan hated shopping for clothes when she was a child. (used)
   When she was a child, Susan _____
   _____.
4 Going for a run is something you do every morning. (go)
   I _____ in the morning.
5 You get annoyed at yourself because you frequently forget your key. (constantly)
   I _____ my key!
6 Your grandfather used to tell silly jokes when you were younger. (always)
   My grandfather _____
   silly jokes when I was younger.
7 Running home from school was something you did every day. (used)
   I _____ every day.

3 Choose the correct sentence in each pair.

1 **a** I use to ride horses when I was young.
   b I used to ride horses when I was young.

2 **a** I have listened to music since I was five years old.
   b I used to listen to music since I was five years old.

3 **a** We went to the same school and every morning she used to pick me up from my house.
   b We went to the same school and every morning she was picking me up from my house.

4 **a** We'll go to the park and hang out by the lake, like we used to.
   b We'll go to the park and hang out by the lake, like we use to.

VOCABULARY Expressing frequency

1 Match the adverbs to words or expressions in the box with a similar meaning. One adverb matches two expressions.

| all the time   every once in a while |
| from time to time   often   seldom |

1 rarely _____
2 constantly _____
3 occasionally _____
4 most days _____

2 Put the adverbs and expressions in brackets in the correct position.

0 My dad ___*constantly*___ asks me how I'm doing at school _____. (constantly)
1 We go _____ to a circus
   _____. (every once in a while)
2 I _____ go to bed after midnight
   _____. (seldom)
3 My best friend and I _____ meet for a chat _____. (most weeks)
4 I _____ read a newspaper
   _____. (every day)
5 I _____ visit an art gallery
   _____. (from time to time)
6 _____ I _____ listen to music. (rarely)
7 My family _____ eats in a restaurant
   _____. (almost never)

3 Rewrite the sentences in Exercise 2 so that they are true for you.

0 *My dad occasionally asks me how I'm doing at school.*
1 _____
2 _____
3 _____
4 _____
5 _____
6 _____
7 _____

⟫ See *Prepare to write* box, Student's Book page 35.

1 Look at the exam task below and think about how you would organise your article. Write these questions and notes into the plan on the right according to where you think the answers fit best.

> A summary sentence or two
> Who is the person?
> What would you ask them?
> Why are they a hero?
> What do you admire about them?

You see this announcement in an international English language magazine.

> **My hero from history**
> Which person from history do you most admire?
> What things would you ask him or her if you were able to travel back in time?
> Write us an article answering these questions.
> We will publish the best articles in the next issue.

Write your **article**.

2 The article on the right contains the four paragraphs in Exercise 1. Number them in the correct order.

3 Is the order of the information in the article the same as in your plan in Exercise 1? What is the function of each paragraph?

Paragraph 1 *introduces the person and says why he's a hero.*

Paragraph 2

Paragraph 3

Paragraph 4

4 Read the article again. Is the style formal or informal? Underline the sentences which indicate this.

PREPARE FOR THE EXAM

Writing Part 2 (An article)

5 Which famous person from history would you like to meet? Use the model in Exercise 1 to make notes, then write your article. Write 140–190 words.

EXAM TIPS

- Divide your article into paragraphs.
- Cover each point from the task in a separate paragraph.
- Include a title to suggest what the article is about.
- Use an informal style throughout the article.

My hero from history

Paragraph 1 introduction:

Paragraph 2:

Paragraph 3:

Paragraph 4 conclusion:

MY HERO FROM HISTORY

All in all, I think the world would be a better place if there were more people like Gandhi alive. His non-violence and his ability to bring different people together for a common purpose would help the world become a happier and more peaceful place. Who doesn't want that?

Believe me, there are so many questions I would like to ask Gandhi if I could meet him! The main thing I would like to know is what he would do to stop all the wars and fighting in the world today. Does he have a solution?

The person from history I would most like to meet is Mahatma Gandhi. He was a famous Indian politician who died in 1948, and I believe he was a really exceptional man. Not only that – he helped India become an independent nation.

I admire him because of his bravery and because of his use of non-violent tecÚiques to achieve his aims. He believed in the power of truth. One of the most amazing things he did was unite people of different religions in India in order to gain independence.

6 TOTALLY EMOTIONAL

VOCABULARY — Expressing emotions

1 Match the words and phrases to the meanings.

1 optimistic ....
2 pessimistic ....
3 over the moon ....
4 furious ....
5 scared ....
6 fed up ....
7 relieved ....
8 depressed ....
9 content ....

a happy that something unpleasant has not happened
b very pleased about something
c very angry
d unhappy and without hope for the future
e frightened
f always believing that bad things are likely to happen
g annoyed or bored by something that you have experienced for too long
h always believing that good things will happen
i pleased with your situation and not hoping for change or improvement

2 Complete the sentences with the words in Exercise 1.

1 I'm really _____ of horror films.
2 I was _____ with the person who stole my bike.
3 I was _____ about winning first prize in the essay competition.
4 I'm really _____ with my brother for borrowing my laptop without asking me.
5 He's feeling _____ about passing his exams tomorrow because he didn't revise much.
6 I'm feeling _____ about passing my exams because I've done lots of revision.
7 I was _____ about finding our lost cat safe and well this morning.
8 I sometimes get _____ about all the bad news I see on TV.
9 She's a very happy person who is _____ with her life.

3 Choose the correct words. Sometimes two are correct.

1 Our new teacher is really good fun. She's always *anxious / depressed / cheerful*.
2 Mum was angry when I got home late last night, but I know that it was because she was *down / concerned / anxious* about me.
3 Jude was a bit *irritated / relieved / content* because I was late again.
4 When my brother wasn't allowed to go on the school trip he was really *content / over the moon / bad-tempered* all day.
5 Our cousins have got a huge dog and my little sister was *scared / fed up / petrified* of it when they visited us.
6 I was really *down / cheerful / depressed* about failing my exams.

4 Find the odd word out.

1 down   depressed   cheerful   pessimistic
2 irritated   concerned   furious   bad-tempered
3 fed up   relieved   optimistic   over the moon
4 content   cheerful   concerned   relieved
5 furious   petrified   scared   anxious

READING

 PREPARE FOR THE EXAM

Reading and Use of English Part 1

1 Read the first three paragraphs of the text and decide which answer (A, B, C or D) best fits each gap.

0 (A) about   B around   C for   D with
1 A left   B missed   C escaped   D avoided
2 A example   B enquiry   C experiment D examinatio
3 A nearby   B about   C throughout D around
4 A state   B shape   C position   D frame
5 A grow   B increase   C climb   D spread
6 A goals   B reasons   C points   D objects
7 A sensitive   B alive   C informed   D aware
8 A slightly   B almost   C hardly   D little

 EXAM TIPS

- If you don't know the answer, try to decide which options do not fit the gap and choose a different one.
- Read the whole text through again to check it makes sense.

Happily bored!

Have you ever complained **(0)** _about_ being bored? Most of us have. Many people think of boredom as something to be **(1)** _____, but being bored can actually lead to great things.

Here is an **(2)** _____ for you to try. Just do nothing for a moment. Observe your thoughts. Your brain isn't doing nothing, is it? It's listening and watching, processing everything **(3)** _____ you, and it may seem quite busy. Your brain is in _Beta mode_. In this **(4)** _____, we act and get things done. Beta brainwaves **(5)** _____ when we are learning, talking or excited. They help us to focus and achieve **(6)** _____ .

Now try being truly bored. Just sit there and try not to think of anything. Gradually, you may notice that your thoughts become less busy. You may become **(7)** _____ of the little sounds and events that surround you. You may begin to think things that had never crossed your mind before. Or you might **(8)** _____ think at all.

When your brain is this inactive, you are said to be in _Alpha mode_. Alpha waves happen when we are very peaceful or relaxed. Our breathing slows. People who spend more time in this state are more likely to daydream, and tend to fall asleep and stay asleep more easily. They might also get less stuff done!

Scientists use a special electronic device to measure brain activity and they can tell whether the brain is in Alpha or Beta mode. Everyone's brainwave activity changes all the time, depending on what they are doing or feeling.

Famous creative thinker Steve Jobs, who co-founded Apple Computers and directed the development of iPads and other new tecÚology, said, 'Boredom allows us to experience curiosity, and out of curiosity comes everything.' He spent many productive hours being bored, and ended up having some pretty amazing ideas.

Scientist Albert Einstein said, 'The monotony of a quiet life stimulates the creative mind.' Just imagine him sitting there with nothing to do, twiddling his thumbs and daydreaming. Do you think young Albert would have had the flashes of inspiration which led to his famous theories if he'd had a mobile phone or computer with games on it back in 1903? Or would he have been too busy trying to reach the next stage in his favourite game?

You didn't know daydreaming was a valuable activity, did you? Many large companies, like Google and Pixar Animation, see creativity as a major business advantage, and they reward their most creative daydreamers for coming up with original ideas. They even have special rooms for encouraging daydreaming, complete with comfortable sofas. People that work at these companies are encouraged to relax and stare into space sometimes, because the companies can see what great ideas come out of these daydreaming sessions. Employees should be careful that they don't actually fall asleep though.

It can be hard to find the time to be bored. If you are lucky enough to have quiet time or simple, repetitive jobs to do, enjoy those moments of boredom. You might have an inspiring thought while you are peeling potatoes, or come up with the next brilliant idea for a story while you're watching the rain run down the window. And that's not boring at all, is it?

2 Are the sentences true or false, or is there no information given in the text?

	True	False	Not given
1 The brain is more active in the Beta state.			
2 Some people are always in the same brain state.			
3 Steve Jobs was less creative when he was in Alpha state.			
4 Albert Einstein had some very good ideas when he was at work.			
5 Google and Pixar encourage their employees to sleep at work.			
6 People should always try to avoid being bored.			

3 Match the highlighted words in the text to the meanings.

1 the state of being bored _____
2 have pleasant thoughts about something you like or would like to happen _____
3 the feeling of wanting to know about something _____
4 watch something carefully _____
5 piece of equipment used for a particular purpose _____

GRAMMAR be / get used to

1 Complete the conversations with the correct form of *(not) be/get used to.*

0 A: How's your new job in the café?
B: It's OK. I didn't like it at first, but
I ___'m getting used to___ it slowly.

1 A: Why has the cat disappeared?
B: There are too many children in the house, and
the cat _____ it. (not)

2 A: I _____ getting up so early in
the morning. (not)
B: Don't worry, you _____ it.

3 A: What do you think of your new teacher,
Mrs Smith?
B: She's nice, but we _____
being given so much homework! (not)

4 A: Our kitchen is being redecorated, so we
have to eat in a restaurant every night.
I _____ it! (not)
B: I wouldn't like that. I _____
eating good home cooking.

2 Read the situations and complete the sentences
using *be used to* or *get used to.*

1 We moved house from the city to the country. It
was really quiet at night, which was strange for me.
I ___was used to___ hearing the noise of the city
when I lay in bed at night. It took me a long time
to _____ the silence.

2 When I started training with the school swimming
team, it was hard work. I _____
so much exercise! My coach told me I would
_____ it quite quickly, but it
wasn't true. I've been training for two months and
I _____ it yet!

3 Susan became a vegetarian last year. Her mother
was irritated because she _____
cooking the same meal for the whole family. She
didn't want to cook a special meal just for Susan.
But, she soon _____ it. It took
Susan a long time to _____
living without meat, though!

3 Choose the correct verb forms.

1 When I was a little girl, I *used to / was used to* have
a red skateboard.
2 We don't think we'll ever *be used to / get used to*
this cold weather.
3 When I was a child, we *got used to / used to* visit my
aunt in the country every spring.
4 I didn't like these new jeans at first, but I *am being /
am getting* used to them now.
5 They *used to / are used to* living in the United States.
6 My grandad *doesn't use to / isn't used to* having so
many people in the house.

4 Correct the mistakes in the sentences or put a
tick (✓) by any you think are correct.

1 In Sofia there are subways and trains but people
are not used to travel on them. _____
2 I'm afraid I'll have to bring lots of clothes as
I'm not used to living in such a cold place.
_____
3 I can cook very well too, because I am used to do it
when my mother is not at home. _____
4 I got used to deal with people and cooking different
kinds of dishes. _____

VOCABULARY Adverbs: type and position

1 Complete the table with the words in the box.

definitely	from time to time	however
calmly	~~last year~~	nevertheless
nearby	outside	probably	quickly
seldom	until tomorrow	

adverbs of time	*last year*
frequency adverbs	
adverbs of certainty	
adverbs of manner	
adverbs of place	
connecting adverbs	

2 Are the adverbs in bold in the correct position?
Put a tick (✓) by any you think are correct and
correct the others.

0 (Definitely) I will help you with your homework
tonight.
1 I had never been to the cinema **before the
age of 14.**
2 She enjoys **from time to time** going to
the beach.
3 **Probably** it won't take you long to get used
to it.
4 James picked up **calmly** the spider and took
it outside.
5 We got dressed **quickly** and went outside.
6 That's a good computer. It's a bit **however**
expensive.

3 Put the words in order to make sentences.

0 night / we / to a / rock concert / last / went
We went to a rock concert last night.
1 often / drink / I / coffee / don't
_____
2 finish / next week / I'll / my project
_____
3 plays / beautifully / she / the piano
_____
4 probably / this film / won't / the kids / enjoy
_____

LISTENING

1 Read the eight questions in Exercise 2. Write the question number next to what it's asking you to listen for.

main topic ....
speaker's feeling ....
speaker's opinion ....
a detail in the situation ....
a reason for something ....

 PREPARE FOR THE EXAM

Listening Part 1

2 You will hear people talking in eight different situations. Read the questions and underline the main ideas that might help you get the correct answers.

1 You hear a girl talking about her summer job.
How does she feel about it?
A content
B fed up
C concerned

2 You hear a radio announcement about a youth circus.
What are listeners being invited to?
A a performance
B a party
C a talk

3 You hear a girl talking about a race she's just won.
What does she say about it?
A She was used to the feeling of winning.
B She didn't have a chance to celebrate it.
C She was too tired to enjoy it.

4 You hear a boy talking about his favourite TV show.
Why does he like the show?
A It is romantic.
B It is funny.
C It is sad.

5 You overhear a boy telling a friend about teaching football at a sports camp for kids.
How is he feeling?
A surprised at how tired he is
B irritated by his students' behaviour
C relieved that his approach worked

6 You hear two friends talking about a school event.
What is the boy doing?
A expressing a worry about the event
B persuading his friend to go to the event
C explaining the purpose of the event

7 You hear a young woman talking about rock climbing.
Why does she do it?
A It gives her a sense of achievement.
B It satisfies her need to be alone.
C It lets her escape her daily routine.

8 You hear a girl telling a friend about a problem she has with her phone.
What does the girl decide to do?
A ask her parents to buy her a new phone
B buy a new phone herself
C ask the shop to sort out the problem

3 Listen. For questions 1–8, choose the best answer (A, B or C). Then listen again and check your answers.

05

 EXAM TIPS

- Read the questions carefully before you listen and underline the main ideas in them.
- Identify any functions the questions may be focusing on, for example the speaker's purpose or agreement between the speakers.
- Listen to the whole extract before you choose your answer.

VOCABULARY — Verbs of movement and sounds

1 Match the words in the box to the meanings.

> kneel   lean   mumble   rush   sigh
> slap   swing   tap   tremble   wander
> whisper   whistle

1 move the top part of your body in a particular direction

2 knock or touch something gently ....

3 hurry or move quickly somewhere ....

4 go down into a position where both knees are on the ground ....

5 hit someone with the flat, inside part of your hand ....

6 move smoothly backwards and forwards ....

7 walk slowly in a relaxed way ....

8 speak too quietly and not clearly enough for someone to understand you ....

9 make a sound by breathing air out through a small hole made with your lips ....

10 breathe out slowly and noisily, often because you are annoyed or unhappy ....

11 speak extremely quietly so that other people cannot hear ....

12 shake slightly, usually because you are cold, scared or emotional ....

2 Choose the correct words.

> I was sitting at my desk in the maths lesson yesterday when the boy behind me ¹ *swung / leant* forward and ² *tapped / rushed* me on the shoulder.
> 'Can you hear that noise?' he ³ *trembled / whispered*.
> 'No, I can't hear anything,' I replied, and tried to get back to my maths problems.
> But then, I did hear something, outside in the corridor. Someone was ⁴ *mumbling / whistling* a tune, and it was getting louder. Suddenly the classroom door ⁵ *swung / slapped* open and a man with a pot of paint in each hand ⁶ *knelt / wandered* into the room
> 'Is this the dining hall?' he asked, obviously in a hurry. Our teacher, who was in a bad mood anyway, ⁷ *leant / sighed*.
> 'Does it look like the dining hall?' she asked.
> 'No, no, I suppose not,' ⁸ *mumbled / swung* the man — and he turned around and ⁹ *slapped / rushed* out of the door.
> Everyone was laughing. 'Silence!' our teacher shouted, ¹⁰ *trembling / wandering* with anger. 'Get back to work!'

READING

 PREPARE FOR THE EXAM

Reading and Use of English Part 5

1 You are going to read an article about a young author. For questions 1–6, choose the answer (A, B, C or D) which you think fits best according to the text.

1 What is the author of the article doing in the first paragraph?
A listing some of Emily Franklin's achievements
B explaining how to recognise artistic ability
C examining the topic of literature
D asking Emily Franklin questions

2 How do Emily's parents feel about her writing?
A worried that it might interfere with her education
B proud of the role they played in her success
C confident that she will write a bestseller
D surprised that she has done so well

3 In line 23, what does the author mean when he says the Franklins take a 'hard-headed approach to life'?
A They are constantly looking for opportunities.
B They are hopeful about the future.
C They seldom change their minds.
D They are practical and realistic.

4 What does 'it' refer to in line 33?
A success
B advice
C her novel
D good luck

5 The author of the article thinks that Emily's novel
A should be shorter.
B is an excellent first attempt.
C would make a good film.
D is not on the same level as some similar novels.

6 What is Emily's main reason for writing her novel?
A to entertain her friends
B to make her readers think
C to achieve financial success
D to try to copy great writers of the past

YOUNG NOVELIST

How do you know if you have got literary talent? Is it because your school report talks about your wonderful way with words? Do you amaze and amuse your friends with your stories and poems? Maybe you entered and won a short story competition at the age of eleven? In the case of Emily Franklin, it is all of those things – plus the fact that she has just signed a publishing contract for her first novel. 'I still don't quite believe it, though,' she says. 'It's too much like a dream come true.'

Emily's parents knew there was something special about her from a young age. 'I started writing when I was five, and they were always very encouraging,' she says. At that age, she used to write little poems and short stories, which they enjoyed. Then, when she started writing a novel at the age of 14, her parents told all their friends, but they never believed it would be published. 'So you can imagine their reaction when I told them it had been accepted. Mum started crying and Dad didn't say anything – he just gave me a big hug.'

Of course, nobody knows how her novel – a fantasy set in a world of dragons and magic called *Magical Beast* – will go down with readers and critics. As a family, the Franklins
23 have always taken a very **hard-headed approach to life**, so they're not expecting Emily to be the new J. K. Rowling. 'The fact that she's got this far is incredible,' says her father, Mark. 'But she's not going to be giving up school anytime soon, regardless of how well it sells!'

Does Emily have anything to say to aspiring young authors? 'When the news about me getting published got around, quite a few people contacted me asking for advice,' she says. 'But I'm only sixteen. I wrote one novel, and got lucky – so I'm not sure that I'm
33 qualified to offer **it**!' Nevertheless, when I press her, she does have something useful to pass on: 'Just write,' she says. 'Don't wait until inspiration arrives, or you may never get anything done!'

So what is the book like? Emily's publisher provided me with an advance copy, which I read in the week before I met her. The plot centres on the adventures of three friends as they make their way through a strange land in search of a magic statue. It's quite derivative – a cross between *Harry Potter* and *Lord of the Rings* – but it's no worse for that. At 400 pages, it's not a quick read, but it's a real page-turner and remarkably well written. The action comes thick and fast – in fact, the whole thing is crying out for the big-screen treatment. Whether or not that happens depends on how well it sells – but one thing is for sure: if Emily writes another novel, I'll definitely read it.

When I ask her about her influences, she admits that she is a big fan of the *Lord of the Rings* films. She has read the *Harry Potter* books, but they are not really to her taste. 'I prefer the classics – Dostoevsky, Conrad – they're my heroes.' Originally, her novel started as a series of chapters for the amusement of her friends, but it soon grew into something more ambitious. 'I strongly believe young people can handle big themes. I want my readers to consider topics like freedom and identity. You need to be yourself in the world.' It looks like, for Emily, being herself could make her quite wealthy one day.

2 Read the questions again. Underline the parts of the article which gave you the answers.

3 Match the highlighted words in the text to the meanings.

1 in a way that makes you feel surprised ....
2 without being affected or influenced by anything else that happens ....
3 subjects of a book, talk, film, etc. ....
4 connected with literature ....
5 something you say, feel, or do because of something that happened ....

1 Match the sentence halves.

1 She was walking through the woods
2 By the time we got to the stadium,
3 His hair was wet because
4 I took off my coat
5 The burglar got in easily because
6 We had been travelling for hours
7 As soon as she had spoken,
8 When we arrived at the party,

a the match had already started.
b when she heard a scream.
c she regretted it.
d we hadn't locked the back door.
e everyone was dancing.
f and sat down on the sofa.
g before we decided to stop and rest.
h he had been swimming in the river.

| 1 ____ | 3 ____ | 5 ____ | 7 ____ |
| 2 ____ | 4 ____ | 6 ____ | 8 ____ |

2 Complete the sentences with the past simple, past perfect simple or past perfect continuous form of the verb in brackets.

1 By the time our meal arrived we _____ (wait) for an hour and a half.

2 My parents _____ (not believe) me when I told them I _____ (pass) every one of my exams.

3 She _____ (put on) her raincoat, _____ (pick up) her umbrella, and _____ (leave) the house.

4 They _____ (train) all morning in the gym, which is why they _____ (be) exhausted.

5 I _____ (only sit) down for a couple of minutes when my brother _____ (come) in and _____ (ask) me to help him fix his bike.

6 We _____ (run) for an hour when the storm _____ (begin).

7 Everyone _____ (already start) eating by the time we _____ (get) home.

8 Even though we _____ (never meet), I _____ (recognise) him from his Facebook page.

9 Luisa _____ (write) short stories since she _____ (be) a child, and then her favourite magazine _____ (offer) to publish one of them.

10 Before I _____ (have) the opportunity to book tickets for the concert, they _____ (all sell) out.

3 Write one sentence from the notes, using the correct tenses.

0 when / we / arrive at cinema / 7.40 / film / start
When we arrived at the cinema at 7.40, the film had started.

1 the teacher / talk / fire alarm / ring

2 Karen / learn Spanish / two years / when / move to Argentina

3 I leave home / run for the bus / and arrive at school / on time

4 we get home / Dad finish preparing dinner

4 Choose the correct sentence in each pair.

1 a I received your letter this morning.
  b I had received your letter this morning.

2 a He saw a woman he never met before.
  b He saw a woman he had never met before.

3 a I enjoyed it a lot and would do it again.
  b I had enjoyed it a lot and would do it again.

4 a It was the first time I went to the cinema.
  b It was the first time I had been to the cinema.

1 Make five time phrases then write them next to their definitions.

1 for some	no time
2 before	long
3 the week	on end
4 for weeks	before last
5 in	time

a quite soon _____
b very quickly _____
c two weeks ago _____
d for several weeks _____
e for a long period _____

2 Choose the correct time phrases.

1 Tim had no trouble settling in to his new school – he got used to it *for some time / in no time.*

2 I went to bed at 11 o'clock and *before long / for days on end* was fast asleep.

3 She had wanted to meet her pen friend *for some time / in no time* and was pleased to get the chance.

4 They finished all their exams *the week before last / for weeks on end.*

5 We waited for the weather to improve *before long / for days on end* but it never did.

A story

>> See *Prepare to write* box, Student's Book page 45.

1 Look at the exam task and make notes below for a possible story.

You have seen this notice on an English-language website.

Stories wanted

We are looking for stories for our new English-language magazine for young people. Your story must **begin** with this sentence:

When I opened the front door, I found a small package with a note attached to it.

Your story must include:
- a key
- a surprise

Write your **story**.

What did the note say?

_____

What was in the package?

_____

What happened next?

_____

How did you feel?

_____

2 Read the story, ignoring the gaps. Does it contain any of your ideas? Does the story include the ideas mentioned in the task?

When I opened the front door, I found a small package with a note attached to it. I ¹_____ (pick) it up and ²_____ (read) the note. All it said was, 'Enjoy!'

How mysterious! Who ³_____ (leave) this package on my doorstep? What was inside? I didn't waste much time. I ⁴_____ (take) the package into the kitchen, ⁵_____ (put) it on the table, and ⁶_____ (open) it. Inside was a key, and another piece of paper. On the paper, somebody ⁷_____ (write) the words, 'Go into the garden.'

I picked up the key and examined it. It was quite small – too small to be a door key. What could it be for? I went to the kitchen window and looked out towards the garden. It ⁸_____ (rain) slightly, so I ⁹_____ (not want) to go outside. But I put on my shoes and opened the back door.

And then I saw it. Behind the shed was a motorbike. The key was a motorbike key! Suddenly the shed door opened and my mum and dad jumped out. 'Surprise!' they shouted. 'Happy Birthday!' I was speechless.

---

3 Rewrite your notes from Exercise 1 so they are about the story.

What did the note say? (paragraph 1)
Enjoy!
_____
What was in the package? (paragraph 2)

_____
What happened next? (paragraph 3)

_____
How did you feel? (paragraph 4)

_____

4 Now write the verbs in brackets in the story in the correct form.

 PREPARE FOR THE EXAM

Writing Part 2 (A story)

5 Write your story. Use the questions in Exercises 1 and 3 to plan your story. Think about the pronouns and tenses you will need to use. Write 140–190 words.

 EXAM TIPS

- Read the first sentence and think about the situation before you start writing.
- Plan the events in your story, making sure there is a link to the first sentence.
- Be careful to use the correct pronouns and tenses.
- Check your story has a beginning, a middle and an end.

8 A GREAT PLACE TO LIVE

VOCABULARY Community

1 Complete the crossword, using the clues to help you.

Across
1 belonging to or relating to a city
5 seeing or communicating with each other a lot
9 comfortable and informal, not tense
11 fashionable
12 relating to the countryside

Down
2 far away from anywhere
3 cheap enough for most people
4 having only houses and not offices or factories
6 in the central part of the city
7 friendly to visitors
8 connected with industry and factories
10 containing people from many different cultures

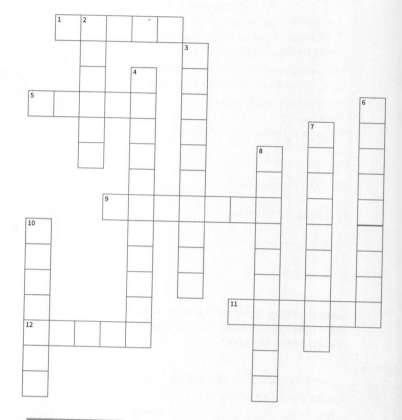

2 Choose the odd one out in each group of words.

1 inner city	rural	urban
2 industrial	close	welcoming
3 diverse	urban	inner city
4 residential	remote	industrial
5 remote	affordable	rural
6 inner city	relaxed	trendy

3 Complete the sentences with the words in Exercise 1.

1 You won't find many offices or factories here. This is a _____ area.
2 I wouldn't like to live in a really _____ place; I like having cafés and shops nearby.
3 London is a very _____ city, where people from all over the world live and work.
4 Everyone looks so young and fashionable here, and the shops are so modern – this part of San Francisco is such a _____ place.
5 The trouble with living in an _____ area is that the factories can be quite noisy and polluting.
6 I'd like to live in the _____ city area, but it's too expensive. I need to find somewhere more _____ .
7 This is a very _____ community where the people look out for each other.
8 My aunt and uncle decided to leave the city and _____ life behind, and they found a lovely village in a _____ area, surrounded by forests and mountains.

READING

 PREPARE FOR THE EXAM

Reading and Use of English Part 7

1 You are going to read four reports by teenagers who have gone on a school trip to a city. For questions 1–10, choose from the four people A–D. The people may be chosen more than once.

Which person
1 was uncomfortable in their accommodation? ....
2 regretted a decision they made? ....
3 overcame an initial fear? ....
4 expected things to be more expensive? ....
5 intends to repeat the experience soon? ....
6 was surprised by how welcoming people were? ....
7 was pleased to make several new friends? ....
8 thought the place they stayed in was very trendy? ....
9 was impressed by the diverse character of the city? ....
10 recommends doing something they did? ....

School city trips

A

I wasn't that keen on going on the London trip with my school. It was a whole weekend away from home, which was something I'd never done before, and I was a bit anxious. But I needn't have worried. We were so busy having fun that I didn't have time to miss anyone! Our school is in quite a remote part of England, and the thing that really struck me about London was the huge variety of people there from lots of different cultures. Just walking around the shops, I heard so many different languages spoken. Our hotel was nice enough. The staff made us feel welcome. I shared a room with two friends, and we stayed up rather late chatting, so we were exhausted the next day. One thing I will say is, London isn't cheap! Next time I'll bring more money – but I'm not sure when that will be.

B

The school trip to Lisbon was a fabulous experience. There were about twenty of us, plus four teachers on this week-long visit. Students from the year above and below were among us, and I got pretty close to quite a few people I'd never spoken to much before, so that was a bonus. For accommodation, we were split into six groups and we each stayed in the home of a different host family. I thought that might be a bit awkward, but the family we stayed with made us feel so at home and put us at ease immediately. I couldn't believe how lovely they were. During the day we met up with the rest of the group and did sightseeing and stuff. The food was amazing, and considering Lisbon is a capital city, surprisingly reasonable. I hope to go back sometime in the future.

C

Vienna wasn't my first choice of city to go to on the school trip – but we had a vote, and it was the most popular choice, so I decided to go along anyway. I'm glad I did. The hostel we stayed in was quite unique. The rooms were decorated with graffiti and modern art – very hip and fashionable. The person I shared a room with was a classmate who I got on fine with, which was a relief. I didn't sleep particularly well, however, as it was mid-summer and the air conditioning wasn't working properly. Apart from this disappointment (the accommodation the school booked wasn't exactly budget class), we did have a great time. What a wonderful city! It's absolute heaven for a 'culture vulture' like me, with such a variety of art and history to experience. I'm going to convince my parents to book us on a trip there this winter.

D

Although Paris is one of the most beautiful cities in the world, the people have a reputation for being a bit unfriendly. So I was a little bit worried about that – but I shouldn't have been, because it didn't matter. There are so many things to do that it is impossible to fit it all in to a long weekend. One day we had the choice of going to see the art in the Louvre, or climbing the Eiffel Tower. I chose the tower, which turned out to be a shame because the weather was poor. Those who went to the Louvre said it was incredible and everyone should go there. Never mind. The next day was better, and I went with a few others on a bicycle tour of the city, which is definitely worth the money if you're ever in Paris with a few hours to spare.

EXAM TIPS

- Read the questions and text quickly to get the general meaning.
- Be careful when you find the same words from a question used in the text – think about the meaning and whether it matches the question.
- If you can't decide between two texts, underline the relevant words in both and return to the question later.

2 Read the questions again and underline the parts of the reports which give you the answers.

3 Match the highlighted words in the reports to the meanings.

1 the opinion that people have about someone or something because of their behaviour or character in the past ....
2 was obvious from the start ....
3 difficult or causing problems or embarrassment ....
4 very cheap ....
5 another pleasant thing in addition to something you were expecting ....

1 Choose the correct options. Sometimes two are correct.

1 The taxi's here. We _____ leave for the airport.
   A 're about to   B will   C may

2 I think you _____ enjoy living in this city.
   A are   B will   C are going to

3 After I _____ to drive, my dad's going to buy me a car.
   A 'll learn   B 'm learning   C 've learnt

4 Have you decided what you _____ study at university yet?
   A 'll   B 're going to   C are about to

5 They _____ be hungry when they arrive – I don't know if they've eaten.
   A 'll   B might   C 're going to

6 I'm not tired yet – I think I _____ watch a DVD before I go to bed.
   A 'll   B could   C 'm about to

7 What time _____ the train leave for London?
   A is   B will   C does

8 I _____ Rachel in town this afternoon, so I'll definitely ask her then.
   A 'm seeing   B might see   C 'm about to see

2 Complete the sentences with the best future form of the verbs in the box.

| answer | depart | finish | get | jump | snow | ~~start~~ |

0 They *are about to start* running.

3 I'll meet you when I _____ this.

1 It _____ tomorrow.

4 He _____ off the cliff.

MAY 7th
7:30
FLIGHT TO RIO

6 The plane to Rio _____ at 7.30.

2 Don't worry, I _____ it.

5 She _____ a taxi, or she _____ a train.

3 Correct the mistakes in the sentences or put a tick (✓) by any you think are correct.

1 We will pick you up from the airport when you'll arrive.
_____

2 I am sure you find lots of interesting things to do during your visit.
_____

3 I hope my suggestion will be useful to you.
_____

4 It's great that you will come to London.
_____

5 We will discuss it when you will come home.
_____

6 I'm going to travel by plane, so I'll book the tickets soon.
_____

VOCABULARY · *as if / as though*

Write sentences to complete the conversations. Use the prompts in brackets and *as if / as though*.

0 A: Oh no! Look at that dog!
  B: (look / attack us!)
    It looks as though it's going to attack us!

1 A: Tony's behaving strangely, isn't he?
  B: (yes / act / win the lottery)

2 A: Why are you phoning a taxi?
  B: (look / the bus / late)

3 A: You don't look very well.
  B: (feel / not sleep for days)

4 A: How did Jane sound when she phoned you?
  B: (sound / not happy about something)

5 A: How was your first day back at college?
  B: (feel / never be away)

6 A: Do you know that girl over there?
  B: (no / but / act / know us)

LISTENING

1 Look at each gap in the sentences in Exercise 3. Work out what kind of information is needed to fill the gap. (Two items from the list are used twice.)

	Gap(s)
a game or sport	
a geographical feature, place	
a task	
an ability	
a qualification	
a type of media	
a food item	
a subject / topic	

2 Read the sentences again quickly. What is Sara's talk about?

PREPARE FOR THE EXAM

Listening Part 2

3 You will hear a talk by a girl called Sara Richardson who was a volunteer on a conservation project. For questions 1–10, complete the sentences with a word or short phrase.

Conservation project

1 It was Sara's interest in _____ which made her want to work on the conservation project.
2 Sara says that the project gave her useful information which helped with her _____ .
3 Sara slept in the camp that was near _____ .
4 Sara did not enjoy _____ when she was on 'camp duty'.
5 Sara missed eating her _____ , which wasn't available.
6 Sara learnt the skill of _____ , which is useful to her in her work at the moment.
7 Sara's camera took particularly good photographs of _____ .
8 During quiet periods, the volunteers would play _____ and chess.
9 Sara mentions a _____ where people are allowed to feed the animals.
10 Sara has produced a _____ about her time on the conservation project.

4 Listen again and check your answers.

EXAM TIPS

- Read the sentences first and decide what type of information is needed in each gap – it is usually a noun or noun phrase.
- You will hear the actual words you need to write in the recording.
- Check your answers when you listen the second time. Be careful to spell everything correctly.

9 A BRIGHT FUTURE

VOCABULARY Collocations

1 Match the two halves of the collocations.

1	achieve	a	the best of
2	go	b	bright
3	have	c	every opportunity
4	have	d	the best in
5	look	e	the worst in
6	make	f	your goals
7	make	g	wrong
8	make	h	a go
9	put	i	the most of
10	see	j	strengths and weaknesses
11	see	k	a difference
12	take	l	an end to

1	4	7	10 ....
2	5	8	11 ....
3	6	9	12 ....

2 Complete the sentences with the correct form of the collocations in Exercise 1.

1 Sally is an optimist. She always thinks the future
   ....
2 You will only .... your
   .... if you work hard.
3 Why do you ....
   to criticise my work? It's very discouraging.
4 The project was a disaster. Everything ....
   ....
5 Although the weather was terrible, and the hotel
   was noisy, we ....
   a bad situation, and had a good holiday.
6 We scored a goal in the last minute, but it didn't
   .... to the final
   result – we still lost the match.
7 I had never tried skiing before, but I ....
   .... when I visited friends in Austria,
   and was quite good at it.
8 He always tries to ....
   people, which is why he is often disappointed when
   they let him down.
9 As a chess player, Mark ....
   .... – he's good at attacking, but not
   so good at defending.
10 Let's try to ....
   our last two days off before school starts again.
11 Unfortunately she broke her leg last year, which
   .... her tennis
   career.
12 I think someone must have hurt Sarah badly – she
   always .... people
   now.

READING

1 Read the article quickly. Would you describe the writer as an optimist or a pessimist?

2 The first sentence of each paragraph has been removed from the article. Choose the one which fits in each gap.

A It's hard to express the feeling I experienced at that moment.
B So that is exactly what I did.
C I'm still selling mobile phones a year later.
D Their shop was located in a shopping centre right in the middle of the city, and I found it easily.
E A year ago I'd left school, I was 18, and I was living in Brussels.
F Then yet another text appeared: how about selling mobile phones?
G I didn't know the average salesman sells only 15 mobile phone contracts a month.

3 Read the article again and choose the correct answers.

1 According to the first paragraph, how did the writer feel when he received his mother's texts?
   A They made him very concerned about her.
   B He realised that she wanted the best for him.

2 The writer finally decided to return to Britain because
   A he couldn't afford to stay in Belgium.
   B he liked the idea of selling mobile phones.

3 How did the writer feel about his training?
   A surprised that it was so brief
   B worried by the amount of reading involved

4 What does the writer mean by 'it was paying dividends' in paragraph 6?
   A providing financial reward
   B bringing good luck

5 What is the writer's attitude to his work?
   A He sees it as an important part of his life.
   B He regards it as necessary to make money.

4 Match the highlighted words in the article to the meanings.

1 strong feeling of excitement and pleasure ....
2 a lot of money ....
3 a person or organisation who you rent a room or house from ....
4 important parts of something ....
5 the words written for and spoken in a film, speech, etc. ....

MY LIFE IN SALES

1 *E* My mother was texting me almost every day about the awful job market in Britain, trying to persuade me to come home and start a university course to give me better job opportunities. However, her ideas were all really dull: train as an accountant, study law, become a teacher. I was living with a group of friends in a flat in the centre of town, having fun. I knew Mum's suggestions were well-intentioned and the result of nights spent worrying about me. However, they didn't exactly grab my attention.

2 _____ Now this made me pause for thought. I actually loved mobile phones. They always struck me as a modern miracle. It's like carrying a video camera, your entire music collection, and a massive library around with you in your pocket. I've owned several mobile phones in my life – maybe I could have a go at selling them? What was more, I had no desire to spend the rest of my life in Belgium, fun as it was, so I informed my landlord and flatmates that I'd be leaving in two weeks and arranged an interview with a new company called Mobiles-r-Us, based in central Birmingham, not far from where my parents lived.

3 _____ The interview went well and I got the job. I had expected to be given some intensive training for this sales role, but the only guidance I received followed immediately after the interview, lasting all of five minutes. Afterwards, the manager opened his drawer and took out a dozen year-long contracts and a sales script. Holding them out to me, he said, 'Read the script and learn it, then come back to the shop tomorrow and start selling those phones.'

4 _____ I was pretty nervous when the first customer of the day came walking through the door. It was a young man, about my age. My boss told me to take care of him, so I approached and repeated what I'd learned the day before. Much to my surprise, he seemed quite keen, and within ten minutes I had made my first sale: a beautiful, large-screened model with a 12 megapixel camera. It was one of the most expensive in the shop!

5 _____ I imagine a footballer has similar emotions when he scores the winning goal in an important match. All I can say is that I felt that I had arrived, that I had found the thing I was good at, and that doing it better and better was what I wanted to do from then on.

6 _____ I soon broke all the records by selling several times that, to everyone from lawyers to cleaners. I was making a small fortune in bonuses! I had always been good at getting people to do what I wanted, ever since I was a boy, and at last it was paying dividends. Soon I was able to move out of my parents' home, and into my own flat.

7 _____ Will I still be doing it in ten years' time? I honestly can't say. It's quite possible that I will get tired of selling mobile phones – even though the tecÚology is moving so fast and features change every few months. It's essential to keep moving if you want to get on. But there is one thing I am sure of: I'll never get tired of the thrill I get when I make a successful sale. That feeling will stay with me until the day I finally retire – why would I ever stop doing something I love?

1 Choose the correct future form.

1 If you keep spending like that, *you'll be spending / you'll have spent* all of your money before we go.

2 Please don't phone me before 7.00 because *I'll have slept / I'll be sleeping* at that time.

3 By the end of this year, the twins *will be going / will have been going* to this school for three years.

4 I'll be free at 5.00 because *I'll be finishing / I'll have finished* all my homework by then.

5 We can't call on Pippa yet; *she'll be working / she'll have been working* on her music project.

6 My grandfather *will be living / will have been living* in the same house for fifty years in December.

7 When we finally arrive, *we'll have travelled / we'll have been travelling* 2,456 km!

8 If you want to talk to Simon, *he'll be studying / he'll have studied* in the library after lunch.

2 Complete the sentences with the future perfect simple or continuous form of the verbs in the box.

arrive	be	build	cook
finish	read	wait	write

1 By Friday afternoon, I _____ this essay for four days!

2 Don't come round at five o'clock on Thursday – I _____ (not) football practice by then.

3 They're having an anniversary party next week. They _____ married for five years.

4 Do you think you _____ this book by the end of the month?

5 Soon, they _____ this bridge for five years – and it's still not finished!

6 I hope Dad _____ dinner for us when we get home. I'm starving!

7 I'm going home in five minutes. I _____ for them to arrive for exactly an hour by then.

8 By this time tomorrow, we _____ at the holiday resort.

3 Correct the mistakes in the sentences or put a tick (✓) by any you think are correct.

1 I have finished my exams in a couple of days and then I'm going to a small island.

2 When the concert will have finished you can interview the conductor of the orchestra.

3 I will be continuing for four days and finish on Saturday.

4 When I arrive, I'll be wearing jeans and a green T-shirt.

1 Choose the correct suffix to make these words into nouns or adjectives. Be careful to make any spelling changes necessary.

Nouns
0	enjoy	*enjoyment*	-ity
1	personal	_____	~~-ment~~
2	relation	_____	-tion
3	satisfy	_____	-ship

Adjectives
4	act	_____	-able
5	benefit	_____	-al
6	remark	_____	-ive

 PREPARE FOR THE EXAM

Reading and Use of English Part 3

2 For questions 1–8, read the text below. Use the word given in capitals at the end of some of the lines to form a word that fits in the gap in the same line.

Friends

The (0) *majority* of people have at least one friend – but how many people have given serious thought to the importance of friends and (1) _____ in their lives? Recent research into social problems such as homelessness, divorce and obesity has found that much of the (2) _____ for these problems is down to loneliness. When you are in trouble, a good friend can offer (3) _____ support, giving you strength and confidence in your time of need. If they are able, they can also give you (4) _____ help.

But friends are not only for the hard times. When things are going well, true friends provide (5) _____. And, of course, it's not just a one-way street. Friends help each other to be the best they can be. Got exams coming up? Forming a study group among friends can make revising much more (6) _____. Training for a sports (7) _____? Train together! Treasure your friends and they will treasure you. They are more (8) _____ than anything you can own.

MAJOR

FRIEND

RESPONSIBLE

EMOTION

PRACTICE

ENCOURAGE

EFFECT
COMPETE

VALUE

 EXAM TIPS

- Read the whole text first, to get an idea of what it is about.
- Look carefully at each gap to decide what type of word – a noun, a verb, an adjective or an adverb – is needed.
- Make sure that the word you form makes sense in the sentence.

>> See *Prepare to write* box, Student's Book page 57.

1 **Complete the table with the linking words and phrases in bold, according to their function.**

1 I enjoy computer games, **whereas** my brother can't stand them.
2 Children today have a lot of freedom **compared to/with** children forty years ago.
3 **On balance**, I think it is better to study for a career rather than study for pleasure.
4 The new stadium will force a lot of people to move. **Furthermore**, the city cannot afford it.
5 This is a badly written essay. **In addition**, it has been copied from the internet!
6 **On the one hand**, I think global warming is causing a lot of damage. **On the other hand**, I'm enjoying the weather.
7 **To sum up**, it is a very bad idea to allow children under the age of 12 to work.

Adding a new point	
Comparing/ contrasting	*whereas*
Concluding	

2 **Read the essay title below and add some information for each note.**

....
....
....
....
....
....

> **'The world today is a much better place to live in than it was 50 years ago.'**
> **Do you agree?**
>
> Notes
> Write about:
> 1 technology
> 2 health
> 3 .... (your own idea)

3 **Read and complete the essay with the linking words and phrases in Exercise 1.**

Many people today, usually older people, think that we live in very bad times, and imagine that everything was much better 50 years ago, [1]........................... many younger people believe that life is much better today than it used to be. So who is right?

[2]..........................., the pessimists look at all the troubles of the world and blame technology. People were friendlier 50 years ago because they did not spend so much time on social media. [3]..........................., families were closer, and used to do things together, like watch TV and have dinner.

[4]..........................., the optimists will point to the facts. Statistics show that there is less poverty in the world today compared to 50 years ago. Health has improved greatly, with average life expectancy now at around 80 years, [5]........................... to the 1960s when it was only 70. [6]..........................., good quality education has become more widespread throughout the world.

[7]..........................., there are valid arguments for and against the idea that the world is better nowadays. [8]..........................., although we have serious problems to deal with, I'd much rather be alive today than 50 years ago!

4 **Your English teacher has asked you to write an essay on the following subject. Read the essay title and write down some information for each note.**

> **'In 50 years' time, the world will be a much better place to live in than it is now.'**
> **Do you agree?**
>
> Notes
> Write about:
> 1 the environment
> 2 education
> 3 .... (your own idea)

 PREPARE FOR THE EXAM

Writing Part 1

5 **Write your essay. Use your notes and give reasons for your point of view. Write 140–190 words.**

 EXAM TIPS

- Use neutral language in the essay (not informal).
- Make sure your essay is quite impersonal – don't use the pronouns *I* or *you* too often, though you are usually expected to give your opinion.
- Learn to use a range of appropriate linkers.

VOCABULARY — Phrases with *in, out of, at, by*

1 Complete the sentences with *in, out of, at* or *by*.

1 I didn't mean to delete the email – I did it _____ accident.
2 We met _____ secret to plan Marta's surprise party.
3 It was completely _____ character for David to lose his temper like that.
4 Please let me know _____ advance if you can't come to dinner.
5 Sixteen people _____ all turned up to watch our first performance.
6 I'll answer any questions you have _____ detail during the class tomorrow.
7 She found out completely _____ chance that her friend had moved house.
8 The car driver admitted he was _____ fault for the accident.
9 Don't give your details on social media websites – they're _____ risk of being misused.
10 The boy on the skateboard appeared _____ nowhere and ran straight into me!

2 Complete the second sentence so that it means the same as the first sentence. Use a phrase from Exercise 1.

1 It wasn't me who caused the fire.
I wasn't _____ .
2 This message has suddenly appeared on my screen.
This message has appeared _____ .
3 I wasn't expecting to see Martin in town today.
I saw Martin in town today _____ .
4 I'll tell you all about my problem later.
I'll tell you about my problem _____ later.
5 Sarah and I met without telling anybody.
Sarah and I met _____ .
6 It was extremely unlike Daniel to lose his temper like that.
When Daniel lost his temper, it was completely _____ .
7 If we lose this match, we might lose the championship.
The championship is _____ if we lose this match.

3 Answer the questions about you.

1 What was the last thing you did in secret?
_____
2 Have you ever done anything out of character? What?
_____
3 How far in advance do you make arrangements for the weekend?
_____
4 How many cousins do you have in all?
_____
5 When was the last time you did something by accident?
_____

READING

1 Read the article quickly and choose the best title.

A Coincidences – magic or maths?
B Great coincidences in history
C There's no such thing as a coincidence

✓ PREPARE FOR THE EXAM

Reading and Use of English Part 6

2 Read the article again. Six sentences have been removed from the article. Choose from the sentences A–G the one which fits each gap (1–6). There is one extra sentence which you do not need to use.

A It was soon revealed that they had been born on the same day.

B Now that would be a real surprise.

C Similarly, people will meet others who look like themselves, and falling babies will land on the same person – albeit very, very rarely.

D And this is where the problem lies, because there usually isn't one.

E As a result, the coincidence becomes much easier to accept.

F This was a remarkable stroke of luck in its own right, but it is only half the story.

G But are they just two chance events, with no special meaning?

Coincidences almost never fail to surprise us. An unexpected meeting in an unexpected location, two **simultaneous** events, a dream that appeared to come true the next day – there are many varieties of coincidence. **1** ☐ Here are a couple of examples for you to consider.

On July 28th, 1900, the King of Italy, Umberto I, was having dinner in a restaurant in the city of Monza. He was surprised to discover that the restaurant owner was also called Umberto and that they both looked and spoke very much alike. **2** ☐ What is more, the restaurant owner had married a woman called Margherita, which was the name of the queen whom Umberto had married on the same day, and the restaurant was opened on the day of the King's coronation. Sadly, the restaurant owner was shot dead the next morning. Then, later that same day, King Umberto I was also shot dead.

Then there is the case of Joseph Figlock, a street sweeper in Detroit, USA, in the 1930s. He was sweeping a street when a baby fell from a high window onto him. The baby survived the fall, and both man and baby were **unharmed**. **3** ☐ The following year, another baby fell from another window onto poor Joseph Figlock as he was passing underneath. And once again, they both survived the event.

So what are we to make of these extraordinary events? One explanation is known as the Law of Truly Large Numbers. This says that with a large enough **sample**, many strange coincidences are likely to happen. Because we never find it strange when likely things occur, we tend to pay a lot of attention to unlikely events. We notice them more, and look for an explanation. **4** ☐ It's just that we humans find it very difficult to understand large numbers.

Considering there are more than seven billion people on the planet, improbable **occurrences** are to be expected. The unlikeliest of events become highly likely to happen somewhere. Even dreams which appear to predict the future can be explained by the Law of Truly Large Numbers. When seven billion people all dream for two hours per night, some of those dreams are bound to 'come true' the next day. **5** ☐

As mathematics professor JoÚ Allen Paulos says, 'In reality, the most **astonishingly** incredible coincidence would be the complete absence of all coincidence.' What? No coincidences at all? Ever? **6** ☐

 EXAM TIPS

- Read the text quickly for its general meaning and read the sentences A–G, underlining the important words.
- Look at the sentences in the text before and after the gaps to find possible links with the sentences A–G.
- Read through the whole text with your answers in place to check it makes sense.

3 Match the **highlighted** words in the article to the meanings.

1 in an extremely surprising way ....
2 not hurt or damaged ....
3 happening at the same time ....
4 things which happen ....
5 a group of people or things being tested ....

1 Choose the correct verb forms.

1 No wonder Jane is angry with you. You *shouldn't / wouldn't / needn't* have forgotten her birthday!

2 It was an amazing show. You *would have / should have / didn't need to* bought a ticket when you had the chance.

3 We *needn't have taken / shouldn't have taken / didn't need to take* any food to the party because we knew there would be lots there.

4 I'm sorry. I *would / should / wouldn't* have told you that I wasn't coming out tonight.

5 She thought she was going to fail, but she *wouldn't / should / needn't* have worried. She passed easily!

6 I *should / would / needn't* have been so disappointed if we had missed your concert last night.

7 We *needn't / should / wouldn't* have run all the way to the station. The train was an hour late!

8 You *shouldn't have / didn't need to / wouldn't have* been so rude to that man!

2 Complete the sentences with *should have* or *shouldn't have* and one of the verbs in the box.

buy	eat	~~lock~~	play
remember	study		

0 She _____*should have locked*_____ her bike.
1 He _____ so much cake.
2 He _____ his umbrella.
3 She _____ so many things.
4 She _____ more.
5 They _____ computer games until 3.00 am.

3 For questions 1–6, complete the second sentence so that it has a similar meaning to the first sentence, using the word given. Do not change the word given. You must use between two and five words, including the word given.

0 It's a pity John wasn't there because he always enjoys parties.   **WOULD**
   John _*would have enjoyed*_ the party.

1 I'm angry that you didn't let me know you were coming to visit this weekend.   **TOLD**
   You _____ advance that you were coming to visit this weekend.

2 We stayed up late that night because there was no football training the next day.   **NEED**
   We _____ to football training the next day, so we stayed up late that night.

3 It was wrong of me to shout at you in public.   **HAVE**
   I _____ at you in public.

4 I regret not having any contact with my primary school friends any more.   **SHOULD**
   I _____ touch with my primary school friends.

5 She could have finished her homework much more quickly if she had wanted to.   **TAKEN**
   She _____ long to finish her homework.

6 I'm glad the children didn't watch that frightening film.   **HAVE**
   That film _____ the children.

EXAM TIPS

- Think of how the key word is commonly used in a phrase or sentence.
- Read your completed second sentence to check that your answer means the same as the first sentence.
- Make sure you have not changed the word that is given.

4 Correct the mistakes in the sentences or put a tick (✓) by any you think are correct.

1 It had been better to stay in bed. _____

2 I wondered how it would be if you hadn't been there. _____

3 It would been OK if he really wanted to come. _____

4 I shouldn't had done this, because I failed the test. _____

5 According to the advertisement, the show should have started at 19.30. _____

6 We had mountain bikes, so we thought that it could be a great idea to visit the forest. _____

VOCABULARY Extended meanings of words

1 Match the words to their 'extended meanings'.

1	boiling	a	stood very still
2	flooded	b	badly affected
3	froze	c	questioned thoroughly or aggressively
4	bright	d	very hot
5	grilled	e	unclear
6	foggy	f	happy and hopeful
7	hit	g	arrived in large numbers or amounts
8	angel	h	a very good person
9	weigh up	i	involving a lot of arguments
10	lift	j	complete or pass easily
11	stormy	k	consider carefully
12	sail through	l	improve

1	___	4	___	7	___	10	___
2	___	5	___	8	___	11	___
3	___	6	___	9	___	12	___

2 Complete the sentences with the correct form of a word from Exercise 1.

1 Of course I'll babysit for your little boy – he's an _____.

2 My understanding of this is a bit _____, because the teacher didn't explain it very clearly.

3 The head teacher _____ the student for half an hour before letting him go.

4 You don't need your coat today – it's _____ outside!

5 The crowd _____ into the theatre when the doors opened at 7.00 pm.

6 The loss of his student grant _____ him very hard.

7 I have a new job and a new flat, so the future is looking _____ for me at the moment.

8 She _____ in fear when she saw the large dog running towards her.

9 The music was so good it really _____ our spirits.

10 Although they have a very _____ relationship, they actually love each other a lot.

11 She carefully _____ up the advantages and disadvantages of taking the course.

12 The exam was so easy I _____ through it.

LISTENING

1 You will hear a man called Rob Mitchell, who works as a party planner, talking about his work. What do you think are the most important things about planning a good party?

🔊 07 **2** Look at question 1 and the underlined key words. Listen to the first part of the interview and choose the best answer (A, B or C).

1 What does Rob say about the job of party planning?
A It's <u>enjoyable but quite stressful</u>.
B It makes <u>going to parties more fun</u>.
C It's <u>not</u> a good job <u>for shy people</u>.

3 Look at this paragraph from the interview and underline the parts which gave you the answer.

> I love it – but that's not to say it's one big party. It's a business, and you have to please the client. Just because you're throwing a party doesn't mean it's party time for you! There's a lot of work and a lot of worry involved, and you really can't relax until the last guest has left, and the venue is cleaned up. But if you don't mind working long hours, then yes – it's a fun job, and even better if you enjoy the social aspects.

✓ PREPARE FOR THE EXAM

Listening Part 4

🔊 08 **4** Listen to the complete interview. For questions 2–7, choose the best answer (A, B or C).

2 How did Rob get started in party planning?
A He was encouraged by his parents.
B A chance meeting led to employment.
C An events company was looking for an artist.

3 What does Rob say about celebrity clients?
A They try to pay less money for their parties.
B They are rather difficult to work with.
C They are less demanding than other wealthy people.

4 What was the problem with monkeys being involved in one party?
A They cost too much money.
B They were a danger to guests.
C They caused a lot of mess.

5 In Rob's opinion, the essential ingredient for a successful party is
A the imagination of the planner.
B the size of the party space.
C the people who attend.

6 What does Rob enjoy most about his job?
A having the opportunity to meet celebrities
B being in an unpredictable situation
C earning a considerable amount

7 What does Rob plan to do in the future?
A Expand into other kinds of event planning.
B Attract more celebrity customers.
C Employ someone to help him.

🔊 08 **5** Listen again and check your answers.

✓ EXAM TIPS

- Remember that you have one minute to prepare yourself for this part before the recording starts.
- Read the questions and options carefully to get an idea of what the speakers will be talking about.
- Underline the important words and listen for the ideas they express.

VOCABULARY — Phrasal verbs: relationships

1 Complete the crossword, using the clues to help you.

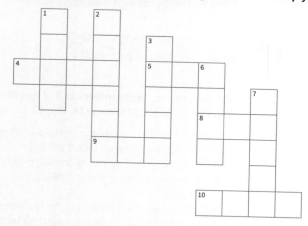

Across

4 If someone looks _____ on you, they think they are better than you.

5 When you go _____ someone, you don't like them anymore.

8 A reliable person will not _____ you down.

9 To '_____ it off' means that you get on well with somebody straight away.

10 If you _____ after somebody in your family, it means you have inherited some of their characteristics.

Down

1 To '_____ up to' someone means to admire them.

2 When you _____ with someone, you end the relationship.

3 If you can _____ on someone, that means you can rely on them.

6 To '_____ out with' means that you have an argument.

7 People who _____ together always support each other.

2 Use a verb from box A and a word from box B to make phrasal verbs. Complete the text with the correct form of the phrasal verb.

A

count	fall	go	hit	let
look x2	stick	take		

B

after	down	down on	on
off x2	out	together	up to

My name's Maria, and I come from a very close family – we always
¹ _____ . My mother is my role model – I really ² _____ her. I think I ³ _____ my mother as she's quite shy and has only two really close friends. I'm quite shy and don't make friends easily either, but when I do become friends with someone, I'm very loyal. You can always ⁴ _____ me to stand by you in your time of need. I will never ⁵ _____ you _____ ! I don't like people who ⁶ _____ others and think they're better than them. If you do that, we will probably ⁷ _____ with each other. We might get on with each other at first; maybe we'll ⁸ _____ it _____ because we both like the same music or something. But I will ⁹ _____ you very quickly if I hear you talking about somebody else in an unpleasant way!

Please leave a message below if you want to chat.

Maria

READING

PREPARE FOR THE EXAM

Reading and Use of English Part 2

1 Read the first two paragraphs of the article. For questions 1–8, think of the word which best fits each gap. Use only one word in each gap.

EXAM TIPS

- Look at the words before and after each gap to help you decide what type of word is needed.
- The words may be part of a phrasal verb or another fixed phrase.
- If you think of two or more possibilities, try them and see which one fits best.

2 Read the rest of the article. What other animals are mentioned?

ANIMAL FAMILIES

'All happy families are alike,' wrote the Russian author Leo Tolstoy, 'but every unhappy family is unhappy in its **(0)** _own_ way.' He was talking about human families, of **(1)** _____ – but if he had turned his attention to the animal kingdom, he would **(2)** _____ found a huge variety of happy families, some of **(3)** _____ raise children very differently to the way humans have done throughout history.

A strong candidate **(4)** _____ the most human-like family in the animal kingdom is the Adelie penguin. The mother and father start by working together to build a nest **(5)** _____ the female will lay her egg. These nests are built with stones to keep the egg off the ice-cold ground of the Antarctic. Then the parents **(6)** _____ turns sitting on the egg. One of them goes off to feed, while the **(7)** _____ stays behind. When the baby is finally born, they once **(8)** _____ share the duties of going fishing and babysitting.

In contrast to this model of gender equality, African elephant females do nearly all the work of raising children. But at least they do not have to do it alone. A herd of elephants is made up mainly of adult females and their offspring. Each herd is ruled by an older female, called the matriarch, and all the adults help with looking after the youngsters. Adult male elephants are solitary creatures, and will usually stay with the herd for about a month before moving on to look for another mate.

Another animal species in which the females do most of the childcare is the Galapagos sea lion. In this case, the father does not abandon his family. A single adult male, the father of all, guards the beach, which is home for up to 30 mothers and their children. Remarkably, these groups, known as 'rookeries', operate a nursery-care system. A mother can leave her child to play with the other kids while

they are all supervised by other females. The mothers take it in turns to do the babysitting.

Our closest animal relative, the chimpanzee, raises families in a tight social structure, with particularly strong bonds forming between the mother and her offspring. Long after an infant has fully grown, they will continue to show affection for their mother – even helping to care for her when she gets old. Chimpanzees live in groups ranging in size from 15 to 150 members and, unlike elephants, these groups are dominated by the males. However, the fathers play very little part in their children's upbringing, apart from hunting and sharing food.

So what can we learn from the study of family structures in the animal kingdom? In the huge variety of roles played by mothers, fathers and social groups, there is one aim common to every species: the well-being of the children. It seems that a family which can achieve this is a happy family – in its own unique way.

---

3 Read the text again and answer the questions with *P* (penguins), *E* (elephants), *S* (sea lions) or *C* (chimpanzees).

In which animal family ...
1 is childcare shared equally?   _P_
2 is a female the boss?
3 do females share the work?
4 do children maintain a long relationship with a parent?
5 does the father look after several females?
6 do males provide food?

4 Match the highlighted words in the article to the meanings.

1 the state of being healthy, happy, and comfortable   _____
2 the way that a parent looks after and teaches a child   _____
3 the child of a person or animal   _____
4 watched to make certain everything is done correctly, safely, etc.   _____
5 leave and not return   _____

GRAMMAR Relative clauses

1 Put brackets around the pronouns that can be left out. If the pronoun can't be left out, write a tick (✓).

0 The book (that) I read last week is going to be made into a film.
1 Is that the man who found your laptop?
2 The steak that I ate last night wasn't very good.
3 Are those the children whose teacher is from Brazil?
4 We didn't enjoy the film that we watched last night.
5 This car, which we bought last summer, is very slow.
6 My best friend, who I've known since we were at primary school, is moving to France.

2 Complete the sentences with *who* or *which*. If the pronoun can be left out, put it in brackets.

1 My uncle, _____ writes horror novels, lives in America.
2 We're looking for a house _____ has four bedrooms.
3 Tell me about the last football match _____ you played in.
4 My grandmother doesn't trust people _____ can't cook.
5 Did you ever meet that penfriend _____ you were writing to?
6 My bike, _____ I bought with my birthday money, has been stolen.

3 Match 1–6 to a–f, then join them with *when, where, which, who* or *whose* to make sentences with defining relative clauses. Make any other changes necessary.

1 A redhead is a person …
2 Moscow is the city …
3 I'll never forget that time …
4 This is the house …
5 There aren't many taxi drivers …
6 There's that boy …

a It's famous for the Kremlin.
b We went to the seaside in the rain.
c His father teaches at my college.
d My grandfather was born here.
e Their hair is red.
f They have never had an accident.

1 *e* A redhead is a person whose hair is red.
2 _____
3 _____
4 _____
5 _____
6 _____

4 Correct the mistakes in the sentences.

👁 1 You are lucky because I've got the information who you need about the new art class. _____
2 You will go to the village, who has a little supermarket, and buy some food. _____
3 One morning we went to the beach wich was about 30 minutes from our campsite. _____
4 Tina had dreamed of winning a ballet contest since she was five years old, that was when she started her lessons. _____
5 She is the actress which is in the new *X-Men* movie! _____

VOCABULARY Compound adjectives

1 Complete the text with the words in the box.

| balanced | behaved | confident |
| grown | organised | tech |

My best friend's mother is quite strict when it comes to parenting. When the children were young, they were always punished when they were [1] badly _____, and rewarded when they were good. Their lives were very [2] well _____, with strict times for going to bed and getting up in the mornings. No computers or [3] high-_____ equipment were allowed in their rooms. Their mother was also careful to provide them both with a [4] well-_____ diet. It seems to have worked, because now that my friend and his sister are [5] _____ up, they are very mature and [6] self-_____ young adults.

2 Combine one word from each column to make compound adjectives. Then match them to the definitions.

middle-   distance
well-   aged
last-   term
long-   paid
short-   built
well-   minute

1 having a large, strong body _____
2 travelling between two places that are a long way apart _____
3 done at the latest possible opportunity _____
4 in the middle of your life before you are old _____
5 earning a lot of money _____
6 relating to a short period of time _____

An article (2)

>> See *Prepare to write* box, Student's Book page 67.

1 **Look at the questions in the exam task. Make notes of your answers.**

....

....

....

You have seen this announcement on an English-language website for students.

> **My perfect home**
> If you and your family could choose to have a home anywhere in the world, where would it be? What would it be like? How would it be different from your current home?
> The best articles will be published here on our website.

Write your **article**.

2 **Read the article. Has the writer answered all the questions? Which paragraph answers which question? Are any of the answers similar to yours?**

My perfect home

A My perfect home would be a large flat in the centre of a big city. Moving to New York is a dream of mine. It's so beautiful and exciting. Everything we need would be nearby – shops, restaurants, cinemas and schools – and we'd have interesting neighbours. Maybe they'd even be famous! How cool would that be?

B The flat would have four bedrooms – one for my parents, and one each for me and my sister. The fourth bedroom is for friends who are visiting. I'm sure there would be lots of friends coming to see us if we had a fantastic flat in New York! Did I mention there would also be a balcony with a view over the rooftops of the city? Wouldn't that be awesome?

C Of course, this perfect home is quite different from where we live now. At the moment we are living in a small house in a small town. The worst thing is, we don't have a spare bedroom. So although there are some OK places in my town which I would show you if you came to visit, you'd have to sleep on the sofa. If I were you, I'd wait until we move to New York!

3 **Read the article again.**

1 Find four informal adjectives.

....

2 Find a sentence which uses an *-ing* form as a subject.

....

3 Find a sentence which uses a structure which adds emphasis.

....

4 Find five sentences where the reader is addressed directly.

....

....

....

....

....

....

 PREPARE FOR THE EXAM

Writing Part 2 (An article)

4 **Write about your perfect home. Use your notes from Exercise 1 to organise your article. Write 140–190 words.**

 EXAM TIPS

- Make notes in answer to each point or question in the task.
- Make your writing more interesting by varying your sentence structures and using informal adjectives.
- Address your reader directly to get their attention.

VOCABULARY Verbs of communication

1 Match the verbs to the meanings.

1 amuse _____
2 cheer up _____
3 congratulate _____
4 highlight _____
5 stimulate _____
6 reassure _____
7 speak out _____
8 spread _____

a promote or increase
b make someone excited and interested about something
c make someone feel happier
d make someone smile or laugh
e emphasise something
f express an opinion on something
g tell someone that you are pleased that they have done something good
h say something to stop someone from worrying

2 Complete the sentences with the correct form of the verbs in Exercise 1.

1 Most of the audience laughed at his joke, but I wasn't _____ at all.
2 We are putting up posters to _____ the news about our new music club.
3 Tonia looks sad. Let's do something to _____ her _____.
4 I tried to _____ him that everything was going to be OK.
5 The documentary intended to _____ people to think about the issue.
6 She felt she had to _____ because it was something she felt strongly about.
7 I'd like to _____ you on winning first prize in the essay competition.
8 They showed us a film to _____ the importance of road safety.

3 Complete the sentences so that they are true for you.

1 I'm often amused when _____
_____

2 _____
_____
always cheers me up.

3 The last time I was congratulated was when _____
_____

4 I once had to reassure somebody about _____
_____

5 _____
is something I will always speak out about.

READING

1 Read the interview with a man who gives free hugs. Choose the correct question for each gap. There is one extra question which you do not need to use.

A Do you get recognised even when you're not doing your free hugs?
B Is that why you go by the false name Juan Mann?
C How did this all start, Juan?
D How do you feel when you give someone a hug?
E What do you do when you're not giving out free hugs?
F So are you worried about how this fame is going to affect your life?

 PREPARE FOR THE EXAM

Reading and Use of English Part 5

2 Read the interview again. For questions 1–6, choose the answer (A, B, C or D) which you think fits best according to the text.

1 Why did Juan Mann decide to give free hugs to people?
A He was inspired by an unexpected act of kindness.
B He wanted to promote human interaction.
C He was upset by recent events in his life.
D He felt in need of reassurance.

2 How did he feel when he first tried giving free hugs in a shopping mall?
A afraid that his intentions would be misunderstood
B confident that he would make people happy
C worried but optimistic about the end result
D aware that he appeared strange to people

3 What does he mean when he describes his employers as 'excitable' (line 26)?
A They are pleased about him attracting business for them.
B They are reluctant to allow him time off work.
C They are nervous about the publicity.
D They are impressed by his abilities.

4 How does he feel about becoming famous?
A excited by the possibility of making money
B unhappy about the attention it will bring
C pessimistic about its long-term effects
D determined not to let it change anything

5 He uses a false name because he wants to
A keep his activities secret.
B feel like a different person.
C remove the focus from himself.
D hide the nature of his mission.

6 What do we learn about Juan Mann in the final paragraph?
A He is grateful to others for his success.
B He is proud of the power of his personality.
C He is embarrassed by the praise he receives.
D He is happy that he is changing the world.

Spreading the love

Today *GladMagz* is talking to Juan Mann, the inventor of the Free Hugs phenomenon. He is set to be interviewed on national TV tomorrow night, and he's feeling pretty nervous.

GladMagz: [1] _____

Juan Mann: I came back from London in January 2004, and my family and friends were spread across the world. I was the only person I knew, and I was all alone. My parents had divorced, I had broken up with my fiancée and my grandmother was sick, and I needed to feel happy. I went out to a party one night, and a completely random person came up to me and gave me a hug. I felt like a king! Six months later I decided to give away free hugs. It would be kind of strange to walk up to a stranger without any form of introduction, and I didn't want to bother anyone, so that's why I held up my 'Free Hugs' sign. My first hug was with a little old lady. I'd been standing in the shopping mall with my sign for 15 minutes and I was terrified. But I'd been hoping that maybe one person out there would take me up on the offer, and the old lady did.

GM: [2] _____

JM: Oh, I just have a little job around the corner from my house – nothing spectacular. I walk away from work and it's all just gone. I don't want to say where, because I'm trying to keep work out of this whole thing – they're really excitable. I guess they're wary about the kind of attention my activities might attract! It's very quiet around here; nothing much goes on, and that's the way I like it. Giving free hugs is one thing that I've gone back to week after week without fail because I know I'm doing something. It doesn't matter that the money's not there and that it's not a career path; what matters is that it makes a difference to somebody's life just for a moment.

GM: [3] _____

JM: It is going to be interesting, but the important thing for me is being able to stay true to myself and keeping my job. People will notice me and I'll be a bit famous for a while, but it will fade in the end. It's exciting, but my life will just go on as it always has and as it always will. If I became a rich and famous 'hugging celebrity' I would still be doing the same thing I do every week.

GM: [4] _____

JM: I keep my real name to myself because the whole thing about a different name is that it's not about me, it's about how it makes people feel and think. I used to say to my friends, 'I'm just one man! What can I do?!' I did feel that I was looking for something that was a little bit more than I'd experienced up to now. I had to do something.

GM: [5] _____

JM: I cut my hair about a year ago because I was getting stopped and hugged at petrol stations while I was buying milk. I felt a bit like Superman and Clark Kent! This has grown beyond anything I ever thought was possible. What started out as a way for me to get a smile out of strangers has turned into this social theory of peace and humanity. I want to go on TV to say thank you to everybody.

3 Match the **highlighted** words in the interview to the meanings.

1 kindness and sympathy towards others _____
2 become less bright, strong or clear _____
3 ended a marriage by official or legal process _____
4 further than, past _____
5 happening or done by chance _____

1 Rewrite the sentences in the passive. Use *by* if it is important to add who or what does something.

0 We may record your call.
Your call may be recorded.

1 You use flour to make bread.

2 People in Brazil speak Portuguese.

3 They don't allow people under 15 to watch this film.

4 Sunlight provides the power in this house.

5 The neighbour's cat bit me on the leg.

6 My brother will arrange everything.

7 Somebody will give you instructions on arrival.

8 People are spending more on smartphones than ever before.

2 Five of the seven underlined clauses in the text can be made passive. Choose which five and rewrite them in the passive.

Last year I experienced real kindness from a girl who has since become my best friend. I had to change school last summer because earlier in the year Dad's company had moved him to an office in a different town, and the rest of the family joined him. That was difficult for me – not only leaving my friends but the thought of having to make new friends. People have often described me as shy and it's true, I find it very difficult to be relaxed with new people. Anyway, on my first day at the new school, someone was showing me into the building when this girl came bouncing up to us and said, 'Hi, I'm Kate, your school buddy. They've given me the job of making you feel welcome here.' Kate stayed with me all day – she sat with me in lessons, she explained how everything worked, she took me to lunch and introduced me to all her friends. Her kindness really impressed me that day.

3 Correct the mistakes in the sentences or put a tick (✓) by any you think are correct.

1 I like to wear clothes which are from cotton.

2 My bicycle has been stolen on the 10th of September.

3 I have a lot of friends, but my best friend calls Maria.

4 They eat special cakes which make for the wedding.

5 I liked the festival very much and I think it should be held again next year.

6 The first restaurant is specialised in seafood.

Causative *have/get*

4 Complete the sentences with the correct form of *have* or *get* and one of the verbs in the box.

build	clean	cut	deliver
look	paint	take	take out

1 I'm thinking of _____ my bicycle _____ pink. What do you think?

2 If your computer isn't working, why don't you _____ Simon _____ at it? He's good at that sort of thing.

3 You'll have to _____ your photo _____ if you're applying for a passport.

4 I couldn't afford to go to the hairdressers, so I _____ my friend _____ my hair.

5 I really need to _____ my school coat _____. It's filthy!

6 She _____ a tooth _____ yesterday.

7 Mum couldn't be bothered to cook, so we _____ a pizza _____ .

8 My friend's parents _____ a swimming pool _____ in their garden next month.

5 Imagine you are very rich. Write four things that you would have/get done for you every day.

I'd have my meals cooked for me by a chef.

both, either, neither

1 Join the sentences with *both, either* or *neither.*

0 He speaks French. He speaks Spanish.
He speaks both French and Spanish.

1 You can have a cake. But if you have a cake, you can't have a biscuit.

2 I don't like cats. I don't like dogs.

3 The film was funny. The film was also scary.

4 Maria doesn't have any time. Donna doesn't have any time.

5 Maybe Greg is lying. Or maybe Dave is lying.

6 He doesn't speak French. He doesn't speak Spanish.

2 Make four sentences about you and one other person. Use *both … and* or *neither … nor.*

Both my brother and I hate football.

LISTENING

1 Read the sentences in Exercise 3 quickly. What is Tonya's talk about?

2 Look at each gap in the sentences in Exercise 3. Work out what kind of information is needed to fill the gap. (Two items from the list are used twice.)

	Gap(s)
an event	
a job	
a topic	
a type of media	
a subject of study	
a personal quality	
a person/organisation	
a number	

 PREPARE FOR THE EXAM

Listening Part 2

3 You will hear a woman called Tonya, who works for an environmental charity, talking to some students about her job. For questions 1–10, complete the sentences with a word or short phrase.

Working at Happy Planet

1 Tonya studied _____ and Spanish at university.
2 After university, Tonya worked as a _____ in Portugal.
3 Tonya was informed by her _____ about the job at Happy Planet.
4 Tonya became the media officer after working at the company for _____ months.
5 Tonya's boss writes about _____ in a weekly newspaper.
6 Tonya gets annoyed when bad publicity appears on _____.
7 Tonya recently enjoyed attending a _____ in New York.
8 Tonya particularly enjoys getting _____ to become involved in environmental activities.
9 In the future, Tonya hopes to be a _____ of online videos.
10 Tonya advises that _____ are essential if you want to become a media officer.

4 Listen again and check your answers.

 EXAM TIPS

- Read the sentences first to get the main idea of the text you're going to hear.
- Make sure the words you put in the gaps fit the sentence grammatically.
- Answer every question, even if you are not sure of the exact words.

VOCABULARY   Leadership and achievement

1 Complete the table with the words below. Some words can go in two columns.

> bossy   conscientious   doubt   drive
> fairly   motivated   put your mind to
> self-esteem   stand out   sympathetic
> target

Noun	Adjective
Verb	Adverb

2 Match the words in Exercise 1 to the meanings.

1 feel uncertain about something
2 understanding and caring
3 in a right and reasonable way
4 be better than other similar things
5 something you intend to achieve
6 always doing your work with care
7 the energy and determination to achieve things
8 confidence in yourself
9 give your full attention to something and try to do it
10 always telling other people what to do
11 keen to succeed

3 Complete the sentences with words from Exercise 1.

1 Do you ever _____ your ability to succeed?
2 Have you set yourself a _____ to achieve before the end of the year?
3 I also have trouble sleeping at night, so I am very _____ to your problem.
4 If you want to _____ in this world, you have to do something that will get you noticed.
5 You must treat people _____ or they will not accept you as a leader.
6 You can achieve anything if you really _____ it.
7 Brian is a very _____ student – that's why he is always welcome on my team.
8 My _____ is quite low at the moment, because I haven't been doing well at school.

4 Answer the questions about you.

1 Who is the bossiest person you know?
2 Who in your class stands out from the crowd?
3 Which of your friends do you think has the highest self-esteem?
4 Who is the most conscientious person you know?
5 What targets do you have which you hope to achieve soon?

READING

PREPARE FOR THE EXAM

Reading and Use of English Part 7

1 You are going to read five reports by people talking about their experiences of leadership. For questions 1–10, choose from the five people A–E. The people may be chosen more than once.

Which person
1 was elected for the leadership role?
2 believes they are a natural leader?
3 benefited from the feedback of people they were leading?
4 believes their success was due to planning?
5 felt uncomfortable telling others what to do?
6 enjoyed the pressure involved in leading?
7 had difficulty getting people to cooperate?
8 likes to lead by setting a good example?
9 is unlikely to repeat the experience?
10 became a leader as a result of an unfortunate event?

EXAM TIPS

- Always read the questions first and underline the main ideas in them.
- Read all the texts quickly for general meaning.
- If you don't understand a word or phrase in a text, try to work out its meaning from the rest of the sentence.
- Choose an answer for every question, even if you have to guess.

2 Read the questions again and underline the parts of the reports which gave you the answers.

LEADERSHIP EXPERIENCES

A   Becoming the coach of my local football team was never part of the plan. I was a keen player, and when an ankle injury put me out of action for a season, I didn't know what to do with myself. So when I was approached by someone from the club to take over as temporary coach, I thought, 'Why not?' The team had been doing very poorly and needed a lot of reorganisation if they were going to survive. It was my first time as coach, so I really wanted to impress. Every game was a battle, but I loved the tension and excitement – in fact I thrived on it. We did OK last season, and I am determined to keep getting better.

B   My first experience of leadership was when I directed the school play. It was a well-known play, which I was looking forward to directing because I had what I thought were some great ideas for it. It turned out to be much harder than I expected. The actors were all literature students with their own opinions, and we didn't always agree on the approach to take. I found that quite awkward at first, perhaps because I didn't have enough confidence in my own vision to push on with it. But some of them had good ideas of their own, which I did take on board – and I think the final production was better for that, ultimately.

C   I started at this school when my parents moved here a year ago. Some people find these changes stressful, but I don't. I'm used to it. The first thing I did was check out the school hockey team. They were in a bit of a mess, near the bottom of the league and lacking motivation. I'm a decent player, and after the first match they made me captain, which is a role I've always felt pretty comfortable in. If my team isn't playing with enough focus or energy, I always raise my own game up a level. I find if you show passion and enthusiasm – and preferably score a goal or two – it rubs off on the team. We haven't lost a game since I took over!

D   My best friend's eighteenth birthday was coming up, and a group of us decided to organise a party for her. As none of us had done anything like it before, and there was a lot to get organised, I volunteered to do the organising. It was a nightmare from start to finish. Food, music, venue, invitations – all these things had to be arranged, so I divided the tasks and tried to get people to work together to achieve our goals. The arguments that broke out about who was doing what were awful! It turned out to be a great party, but if I'm asked to do anything like that again, I'll run a mile!

E   In the final term of my first year at university, our class was divided into teams of five and told to complete a large project. It involved bringing together a lot of topics and ideas, so we thought it would be a good idea if one of us was in overall charge of the project. A couple of us volunteered, but as we only needed one, it was put to the vote – and I won. It was a long term, and the pressure was on to do well. But I'm happy to say that our group ended up with the highest grade because I'd set a strict schedule early on in the project and assigned tasks to people based on their strengths.

3   Match the highlighted words in the reports to the meanings.

1 gave someone a job or responsibility   ....
2 happening soon   ....
3 developed and became successful   ....
4 started doing a job   ....
5 finally

GRAMMAR The passive (2): other structures

1 Complete the second sentence so that it means the same as the first sentence. Use the passive.

0 You must give everyone enough time to finish.
Everyone *must be given enough time to finish*.

1 They're always making me do the boring jobs.
I'm ....
....

2 To be offered a leading role in a film is Amy's dream.
Amy dreams ....
....

3 You must hand in your projects by Friday.
Your projects ....
....

4 Most people think that the new proposals are an improvement.
The new proposals ....
....

5 The judges told David about the prize before they told anyone else.
David was the first ....
....

6 The camp leaders might not allow under-18s to go on the climbing trip.
Under-18s ....
....

2 Complete the paragraph with the correct form of the verbs in brackets.

I've recently started at a new school where students in their final year can ¹ .... (reward) for years of good behaviour by ² .... (give) more responsibility. This involves mainly helping younger students with problems, but it is also possible for other students ³ .... (punish) by the 'student officers' if they notice any discipline issues. Now, I'm sure most students appreciate ⁴ .... (help) sometimes, but no one really wants ⁵ .... (tell) what to do, or punished, by another student. It depends on the student to a great extent, though – you can see that some of them positively enjoy ⁶ .... (hand) the opportunity to act as teachers!

3 Correct the mistakes in the sentences or put a tick (✓) by any you think are correct.

1 It will save a lot of electricity as solar energy is used. ....

2 As could be seen, bikes are really very good: cheap, fast and healthy. ....

3 I believe that this question can be looked at from several points of view. ....

4 It will be prepare by our school cook. ....

VOCABULARY Phrasal verbs with *up*

1 Complete the sentences with the correct form of the verbs in the box.

come	keep	live	make
set	speak	turn	

1 The company was .... up in 2012.
2 Slow down! I can't .... up with you.
3 For homework this week we have to .... up a story.
4 A strange woman .... up to me and started talking.
5 That film just about .... up to my expectations.
6 .... up! I can't hear you.
7 How many people .... up to the party last night?

2 Rewrite the underlined parts of the sentences using the phrasal verbs in Exercise 1.

0 Jo's **starting** a publishing company on the internet.
Jo's setting up a publishing company.

1 I believed his story, but it turns out he **invented** the whole thing!
....

2 What a wonderful show! It **met** all my expectations.
....

3 He speaks so quickly that it is hard to **follow** him.
....

4 I thought they weren't coming, but they eventually **arrived** an hour late.
....

5 You'll have to **talk more loudly** because the microphone isn't working properly.
....

6 The police officer **approached** me and asked me for my name and address.
....

A formal letter or email

>> See *Prepare to write* box, Student's Book page 79.

1 Match the informal expressions to the formal ones.

Informal	Formal
1 I'm sorry …	**a** Could you let me know …
2 I want to …	**b** I apologise …
3 I think …	**c** Dear Sir/Madam
4 Please will you …	**d** I would like to …
5 Tell me …	**e** I would be grateful if you could …
6 Bye!	**f** I believe …
7 Hi!	**g** Yours sincerely / Yours faithfully
8 I'm sure …	**h** I feel certain …

2 Read the following exam task. Underline the main points.

You have seen this advert in your local newspaper.

> **Summer Jobs at Forest Children's Camp**
> We are looking for young people to help with our summer camp for children aged 8–10. We need:
> - children's sports leaders
> - kitchen helpers
> - drama class assistants
>
> Write to us saying which job you are interested in and why you would be suitable.

Write your **letter**.

3 Read the letter, ignoring the gaps. Has the writer completed the task?

1 _____

I saw your advert on the internet and 2 _____
apply for a job
as a children's sports leader.

The job interests me because I wish to have a career as a PE teacher
and 3 _____ that working as a children's sports
leader at your summer camp would be a valuable experience
for me. It will also be useful to earn some money before I go to
university in September. 4 _____ how much
I can expect to earn in this job?

5 _____ that I am a suitable candidate for this
job because I am an enthusiastic player of several different sports, including
volleyball, football, tennis and badminton. In fact, I play for the school team
in all of those sports. I also help to train the younger children at my school in
after-school sports clubs.

6 _____ consider me for this job. I look
forward to hearing from you soon.

7 _____

Karl Barker

4 Complete the letter with some of the formal phrases from Exercise 1.

 PREPARE FOR THE EXAM

Writing Part 2 (A formal letter or email)

5 Write a response to the advert in Exercise 2. Choose one of the other jobs available. Write 140–190 words.

 EXAM TIPS

- Read the task carefully and underline the main points.
- Spend a few minutes making notes on what you need to write about.
- Organise your letter or email clearly in paragraphs.
- Remember to use formal language throughout.

VOCABULARY — Phrasal verbs: transport

1 Complete the crossword, using the clues to help you.

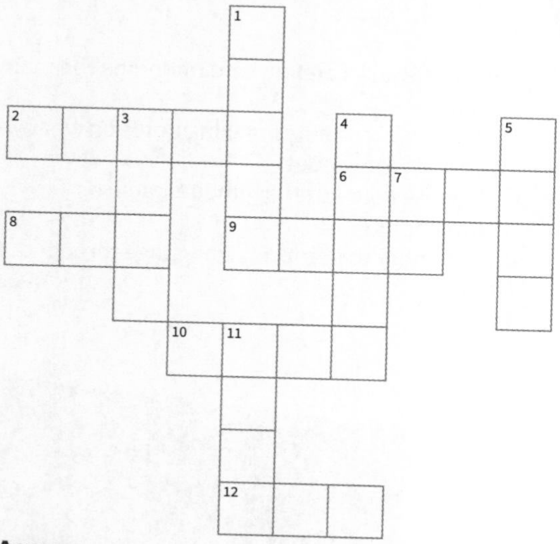

[crossword grid]

Across

2 In a car, you should _____ off when the traffic light turns green.
6 I'm just going to _____ over and let this line of traffic pass us.
8 This train is about to pull _____ of the station.
9 I don't know where to go, so we must _____ up with Louis in the car in front.
10 There's a lot of traffic today. That could _____ us up.
12 I _____ into a parked car as I was driving home yesterday.

Down

1 Something's wrong with the car. I think we're going to _____ down.
3 The train pulled _____ the station ten minutes late.
4 If you don't _____ up, we're going to be late.
5 _____ down! The speed limit is only 50 here.
7 I was walking home when a car pulled _____ alongside me.
11 Oh no! I think I've just run _____ a bird!

2 Match the phrasal verbs in Exercise 1 to the meanings.

1 stop for a short time
2 stop working (of an engine) _____
3 increase speed _____
4 accidentally hit something with a moving vehicle _____
5 hit and drive over something, causing injury or death _____
6 travel at the same speed as _____
7 stop briefly at the side of something, e.g. the road _____
8 arrive at (of a train/car) _____
9 start to move (in a car) _____
10 leave (of a train/car) _____
11 reduce speed _____
12 delay _____

3 Complete the sentences with the correct form of the phrasal verbs in Exercise 1.

1 Can you _____ here please, driver? This is where I want to get out.
2 The train was _____ because of an accident on the railway line.
3 I wasn't looking where I was going and _____ a brick wall!
4 _____! You're driving too fast.
5 A driver _____ next to me and asked me for directions.
6 Our cat was _____ when it was running across the road.
7 I can't _____ with you because you run too fast.
8 The bus driver _____ a petrol station to fill up.
9 We were annoyed when the bus _____ just as we turned the corner.
10 You need to _____ otherwise we are going to miss the train!
11 Do you know what to do if your car _____?
12 We've missed the train – it's _____ of the station now.

READING

1 Read the definition of *ecotourism* in the first paragraph of the article. Choose the 'ecotourist' holiday below.

A a holiday organised by a large company in which a large group travels around, staying and eating in international hotels
B a holiday in which a few people explore a natural area with a local guide, staying in local accommodation
C a holiday to a resort that is staffed by people from all over the world and where you spend 14 days on the beach

2 Match the aspects of ecotourism 1–7 to the paragraphs A–G.

1 It provides direct financial benefits for conservation.
2 It builds environmental awareness.
3 It provides financial benefits for local people.
4 It has very little negative impact.
5 It respects local culture.
6 It involves travel to natural destinations.
7 It is sensitive to how local people are treated by their governments.

ECOTOURISM – a definition

'Take only photographs, leave only footprints.' That was the golden rule for the responsible traveller in the past. But nowadays ecotourism is big business, and The International Ecotourism Society (TIES) has defined it as 'responsible travel to natural areas that encourages conservation of the environment and improves the welfare of local people'. Trips to exotic places are very popular with young people, who tend to be very environmentally aware. So what are the things to look for in a tour operator if you want your holiday to be truly green? According to TIES, there are several aspects to genuine ecotourism:

A These places are often remote areas, whether inhabited or uninhabited, and are usually under some kind of environmental protection scheme.

B Tourism causes damage. Ecotourism tries to reduce the negative effects of hotels, trails, and other things, by using either recycled materials or local building materials, renewable sources of energy, recycling and safe disposal of waste, and environmentally sensitive architecture.

C Ecotourism means education, for both tourists and residents of nearby communities. Before departure, tour operators should supply travellers with reading material about the country, environment and local people, as well as rules for both the traveller and the industry itself. This information helps prepare the tourist to learn about the places visited.

D Ecotourism helps raise money for environmental protection, research and education in a variety of ways, including park entrance fees, taxes on tour companies, hotels, airlines and airports, and voluntary donations.

E National Parks and other conservation areas will only survive if there are 'happy people' around their borders. The local community must be involved with and receive income and other benefits (clean water, roads, health clinics, etc.) from the conservation area and its tourist facilities.

F Ecotourism is not only 'greener' but also tries to be culturally sensitive and have a minimal effect on both the natural environment and the human population of a host country. This is not easy, especially since ecotourism often involves travel to remote areas where small and isolated communities have had little experience of interacting with foreigners.

G Although tourism is often seen as a tool for building international understanding and world peace, this does not happen automatically. Frequently, in fact, tourism helps the economies of undemocratic states. Mass tourism pays very little attention to the political system of the host country or to struggles within it. Ecotourism is much more aware of the political situation.

Most tour operators who can truly be called ecotourism providers are trying to meet as many of these criteria as possible. This is very difficult for anyone operating eco-tours, and it is highly doubtful that any one project or operator can claim to meet them all. However, it does give a base of ideas to work from when looking into whether something is or isn't ecotourism.

3 Answer the questions.

1 According to the article, what does ecotourism try to reduce?

2 What two groups of people does ecotourism seek to educate?

3 What two things benefit financially from ecotourism?

4 What makes it difficult to be 'culturally sensitive'?

5 How easy is it to find an ecotourism provider which covers all of the aspects listed here?

4 Match the highlighted words in the article to the meanings.

1 talking or doing things with other people
2 far away
3 health and happiness
4 money or goods given to help a person or organisation
5 unwanted things

GRAMMAR Reported speech

1 Complete the sentences with the correct form of the verb.

1 We can't help you.
They told us they _____ help us.

2 This is the first time I've tried prawns.
Tom says that this _____ the first time he _____ prawns.

3 They're going to the new club next weekend.
He told me they _____ to the new club next weekend.

4 The soup is much nicer when it's served hot.
Sarah says the soup _____ much nicer when it _____ hot.

5 The original idea was not a practical one.
Mark admitted that the original idea _____ a practical one.

2 Complete the reported speech statements.

1 I won't be going on holiday this year.
Sam says _____

2 She wanted to come to Kenya with us.
He said she _____

3 I've always supported the idea of responsible tourism.
She says _____

4 I'm organising a trip to Japan.
She said _____

5 I can arrange the whole thing for you.
He told us _____

6 Fifty million tourists will be visiting Africa this year.
She claims _____

3 Choose the correct sentence in each pair.

1 a I tell him that you will arrive next week, but I don't think he understood.
  b I told him that you would arrive next week, but I don't think he understood.

2 a It was about three o'clock and I asking the other people if they had seen my sister.
  b It was about three o'clock and I asked the other people if they had seen my sister.

3 a The officer said that David had forgotten to turn his camera off.
  b The officer told that David had forgotten to turn his camera off.

4 a The notice said that ball games were forbidden.
  b The notice told that ball games were forbidden.

4 Write the exact words that these people said.

1 Ted says that air travel is going to get much more expensive.
'_____'

2 She said she had enjoyed her holiday in Nepal very much.
'_____'

3 Jade said she had been trying to reduce her carbon footprint.
'_____'

4 The agent says that the best holidays aren't always the most expensive.
'_____'

5 Polly said she would never forget the week she had spent in India.
'_____'

6 Our teacher told us we'd never have a better opportunity to study abroad.
'_____'

VOCABULARY Reporting verbs

1 Match the verbs to the meanings.

1 agree _____
2 confess _____
3 forbid _____
4 enquire _____
5 insist _____
6 persuade _____
7 point out _____
8 recommend _____

a order someone not to do something
b admit to doing something bad
c say firmly that something is true
d make someone believe that something is true
e tell someone a piece of information
f advise that something should be done
g ask for information
h say that you will do something you have been asked to do

NO
BALL GAMES
· THANK YOU ·

Reading and Use of English Part 4

2 For questions 1–6, complete the second sentence so that it has a similar meaning to the first sentence, using the word given. Do not change the word given. You must use between two and five words, including the word given.

0 'You must not eat anything until dinner time,' my mother told me.
FORBADE
My mother _forbade me from eating_ anything until dinner time.

1 'OK, I'll drive a bit more slowly!' said Mark.
AGREED
Mark .... a bit.

2 'I'm afraid I hit the back of a bus when I was driving home,' said Sue.
RUN
Sue confessed .... the back of a bus when she was driving home.

3 'I recommend you stop briefly at the side of the road every two hours,' said Sara.
PULLING
Sara ....
every two hours.

4 'I'm absolutely certain that I know the way home from here!' said Martin.
INSISTED
Martin ....
the way home from there.

5 'We'll get there quicker if we ride our bikes,' I said.
OUT
I ....
our bikes would be a quicker way to get there.

6 Eventually, we got my dad to see that driving us to the party was a good idea.
PERSUADED
We eventually ....
us to the party.

- This part of the exam tests your grammar and vocabulary.
- Remember to check the number of words you are using. A contraction counts as **two** words.

1 Have you ever stayed in a holiday resort? Make a list of the kinds of job the people who work there do.

....

 10

2 You will hear five short extracts in which teenagers are talking about summer jobs in a holiday resort. Listen carefully to Speaker 1 and choose from the list (A–H) what the speaker says about their job.

A I need to be prepared for the unexpected.
B It can be boring at times.
C I'm finding it easier than I did at first.
D I have to be sociable most of the time.
E It's good practice for my intended career.
F It's more enjoyable than my previous jobs.
G I enjoy certain tasks more than my colleagues do.
H The fixed routine is the best thing about it.

Speaker 1		Speaker 4 ....
Speaker 2		Speaker 5 ....
Speaker 3		

3 Now look at what Speaker 1 says. Underline the words that gave you the answer.

I help with the entertainment in the resort, which covers the nightly stage shows, daily talks and exhibitions, and talent contests. Basically, I'm the person who has to make sure that everything runs smoothly, whether this means finding extra bottles of water for the bands or helping a guest to choose a costume for the talent show. It's impossible to have a daily routine because every day is different – I never get bored! And I seldom get a moment to myself. A major part of my job is to mix with the guests, and everyone knows me by the end of the week. If I'm not actually making announcements on stage, I'm chatting or dancing in the audience. It's all part of what I do.

Listening Part 3

4 Now listen to Speakers 2–5 and choose from the list in Exercise 2 what each speaker says about their job. Use the letters only once. There are three extra letters which you do not need to use.
 11

5 Listen again and check your answers.
11

- Before listening, read the options and underline the key words.
- Wait until each speaker has finished before choosing an answer.
- Remember there are three options which do not apply to any speaker.

VOCABULARY Global issues: nouns and verbs

1 Complete the words in the table, then add the missing words.

	Noun	Verb
1	b _a_ n	_ban_
2	c __ ll __ ct __ __ n	
3		c __ __ __ p __ r __ t __
4		cr __ t __ c __ s __
5	__ l __ ct __ __ n	
6		s __ pp __ rt

2 Match the verbs in the table to the meanings.

1 say that something or someone is bad ....
2 ask people to give money for something ....
3 choose by voting ....
4 forbid ....
5 work together ....
6 actively agree with a person or idea ....

3 Complete the sentences with the correct form of a word from Exercise 1.

1 She's .... for charity.

2 He's talking to his ....

3 Speaking Italian is .... in this classroom – English only!

4 We have an annual .... for president of the Students' Union.

5 They'll be more successful if they .... with each other.

6 She doesn't take .... very well.

READING

1 Read the article 'Do we care about politics?', ignoring the gaps. Which sentence best summarises the main point of the article?

A Young people use social media more these days.
B Young people don't agree on many things these days.
C Young people are less involved in politics these days.

✓ PREPARE FOR THE EXAM

Reading and Use of English Part 1

2 Read the first article. Decide which answer (A, B, C or D) best fits each gap.

	A	B	C	D
0	(A) took	B caught	C made	D held
1	A instance	B thing	C case	D fact
2	A credit	B success	C win	D gain
3	A question	B anxiety	C action	D concern
4	A decline	B refusal	C descent	D dive
5	A animated	B busy	C energetic	D motivated
6	A element	B bit	C part	D piece
7	A lean	B swing	C favour	D tend
8	A shoot	B throw	C launch	D set

✓ EXAM TIPS

- This is mainly a test of your vocabulary, but always check the prepositions and grammatical structure of the gapped sentences.
- Answer every question, even if you are not sure – you might still get it right!

DO WE CARE ABOUT POLITICS?

Gone are the days when students and young people in general **(0)** _took_ an active interest in politics. Nowadays fewer young people vote in elections than used to be the **(1)** _____, and, while some young people still get involved, these days it would be considered a huge **(2)** _____ if even 500 young people met to discuss a political issue. There is no shortage of causes for **(3)** _____, so what is different about the situation today?

Sanal Batra leads the Students' Union at an Asian university. He gives several reasons for this **(4)** _____ in number and importance: these days, students appear to be **(5)** _____ with their own lives, and social media platforms such as Facebook and Twitter have made it easy for them to express their thoughts. Also, he says, young people don't feel **(6)** _____ of the traditional 'establishment' – they have no voice on the larger stage, so **(7)** _____ to focus more on small issues that affect them directly.

Yet this is not necessarily a bad thing, Sanal says. Many students have used social media networks to learn about problems, and even **(8)** _____ specific campaigns against issues that may have an impact on society.

DO WE CARE ABOUT CHARITIES?

According to one study, social media can have an unfortunate effect on both political involvement and charities. The study shows that Facebook and Twitter users are happy to show their support for causes with a 'Like' or a retweet – but then contribute nothing financially. This could be because they are using social media as a means to show others how generous and fashionable they are, without having to put their hands in their pockets.

Report author Kirk Kristofferson said, 'Our research shows that if people are able to declare support for a charity publicly in social media, it can actually make them less likely to donate to the cause later on.' It appears that social media campaigns do raise awareness, but that could be at a cost to how much is raised from collecting money in the high street. Mr Kristofferson argued, 'If the goal is to generate real support, social media campaigns may be a mistake.'

3 **Read both articles and complete the summaries.**

1 Young people are less likely to be politically motivated these days because _____

2 However, they do get more involved with _____

3 Equally, they support charities in a different way as _____

4 So, using social media to promote charities may be a mistake because _____

4 **Match the highlighted words in the articles to the meanings.**

1 when someone takes part in an activity or process _____
2 when there is not enough of something _____
3 particular _____
4 cause something to exist _____
5 give something, especially money, to a cause _____

GRAMMAR — Modals (3): deduction

1 Complete the sentences with *must* or *can't* and the correct form of the verb in brackets.

1 Daniel came first in the marathon! He _____ (train) really hard this summer.
2 Our new head teacher looks very young. She _____ (be) more than 30 years old.
3 It's really cold outside. It _____ (snow) in the mountains.
4 Oh, hello. You _____ (be) Ally's brother. Nice to meet you.
5 Pete trapped his finger in the car door. That _____ (hurt)!
6 Well, I arrived at 8.05 and they weren't there. They _____ (wait) for very long.
7 You _____ (be) delighted when you heard that you'd been offered the job.
8 You _____ (see) Molly when you were in town, because she's on holiday. It _____ (be) someone who looks like her.

2 Rewrite the sentences using the verbs in brackets.

0 I'm sure he's at work today. (must)
He *must be at work today.*
1 Maybe John didn't know about the party (might)
John _____
2 Perhaps Janet forgot to tell you about it. (could)
Janet _____
3 It's not possible that this is your bag. (can't)
This _____
4 Perhaps they met when they were on holiday. (may)
They _____
5 I'm certain that I've seen this film before. (must)
I _____
6 It's possible that the children missed the early train. (might)
The children _____
7 There's no way that was the first time he's played tennis. (can't)
That _____
8 It's possible that Alex is still in class. (might)
Alex _____

3 Correct the mistakes in the sentences or put a tick (✓) by any you think are correct.

1 It must be very interesting. _____
2 It can go wrong, but it can go right too, and if it does, it was worth the effort. _____
3 We wouldn't be able to do 80 km on Saturday because in the mountains it is very difficult and we can get lost. _____
4 My supposed friend turned around and said, 'I don't know you, sir. You might have confused me with someone else.' _____
5 Obviously, it's wonderful to go to a zoo and see the animals from different countries all together, but it mustn't be very nice to be disturbed all day and to have no freedom. _____
6 There are great views throughout the ride, there's an astonishing castle and also a butterfly farm that can turn out to be very interesting. _____

VOCABULARY — Phrases with *in*

1 Complete the puzzle, using the clues to help you.

Across

1 in the _____ of = because of
3 in _____ = happening or being done now
4 in _____ = one after another
5 be in _____ of = agree with or approve a plan or idea
6 in _____ fact = said to emphasise what is true or to give information

Down

2 in _____ = considering the whole of something

2 Complete the sentences with the phrases from Exercise 1.

1 I don't think it will help. _____, I think it might make things worse.
2 We haven't finished decorating yet. Work is still _____.
3 The head teacher called each of the boys to her office _____.
4 My head hurts, I'm tired, I'm hungry – _____, I'm feeling pretty bad.
5 _____ the poor attendance I think we should cancel the meeting.
6 I'm not _____ having another meeting, because it won't do any good.

62   UNIT 15

>> See *Prepare to write* box, Student's Book page 89.

1 Read the four paragraphs of the essay below quickly and put them in the correct order.

1 .... 2 .... 3 .... 4 ....

A However, children are not adults. They are still strongly influenced by their parents. It is possible that a child will be told to vote in the same way as their parents, [1] .... would not be good for democracy. Also, some issues are too complicated to be understood by twelve-year-olds.

B [2] .... that I have presented two sides of the argument, it is clear that we need to find a balance. Perhaps twelve is too young to vote in a government election. But I know some teenagers who are cleverer than some adults, so I believe that they should be allowed to vote [3] .... they reach the age of sixteen.

C The government controls important areas of children's lives such as education and child welfare. It also provides play areas in cities. [4] .... children are young, they are not stupid. [5] .... they are informed about the issues, they should be able to have a say in how the country is run.

D This is a very interesting question, especially considering how the lives of young people are affected by the government of their country. In my country, the minimum age for voting is eighteen. But is this too high?

2 Complete the essay with the linking words in the box.

| Even though | Now | once |
| Provided | which | |

3 Choose the best title for the essay.

A The government has too much influence on children's lives. Do you agree?
B Children should be allowed to vote from the age of twelve. Do you agree?

4 Think about what each paragraph in the essay does. Match the functions in the box to the paragraphs.

summarises the two sides, possibly with a personal opinion

gives details of arguments 'against'

introduces the topic

gives details of arguments 'for'

Paragraph 1
....
Paragraph 2
....
Paragraph 3
....
Paragraph 4
....

 PREPARE FOR THE EXAM

Writing Part 1

5 In your English class you have been talking about pollution in cities. Your English teacher has asked you to write an essay. Write your essay using all the notes and giving reasons for your point of view.

> **'Cars and other motor vehicles should be banned from all city centres.'**
> **Do you agree?**
>
> **Notes**
> Write about:
> 1 pollution
> 2 effects on business
> 3 .... (your own idea)

 EXAM TIPS

- Use a four-paragraph structure for the essay.
- Organise your ideas for and against the topic.
- Try to write in sentences of more than one clause and use a variety of linking words.

VOCABULARY — Advertising: nouns and verbs

1 Match the words and phrases to the definitions.

1 ad break
2 sample
3 appeal to
4 consumer
5 launch
6 sponsor
7 product placement
8 aimed at

a a person who buys something for their own use
b the time on TV or radio used for advertising
c support a person/organisation financially as a way of advertising
d a small amount of something that shows you what it's like
e be attractive to
f intended to influence or affect a particular person or group
g a way of advertising a product by making it appear in a film, TV show, etc.
h make available for the first time

2 Choose the correct words.

1 A local company has just decided to *sponsor / launch* our band.
2 That car manufacturer apparently spent $1 million getting *product placement / samples* in the latest James Bond film.
3 I disagree with advertising that is *sponsoring / aimed at* children.
4 The best thing about some TV programmes is the *samples / ad breaks*.
5 There were people in the shopping centre giving out *sponsors / samples* of a new breakfast cereal.
6 The new edition of Minecraft was *launched / sponsored* yesterday.

3 Complete the sentences with words and phrases from Exercise 1 in the correct form.

1 We need to design something that will .... young adult females.
2 Did you receive a .... of our new product in the post this week?
3 Did you see all the .... in that celebrity's latest video?
4 These food price increases will affect all ....
5 I'm trying to find a new .... for the children's football team.
6 The company is .... its new product at the end of the month. It's .... the teenage market.

4 Answer the questions about yourself.

1 What is your favourite brand of clothing?
2 What do you do during ad breaks?
3 Who sponsors your favourite team?
4 When did you last notice product placement?
5 What was the product?

READING

1 Have you ever thought about a career in advertising? Write five words describing what you think it would be like.

2 Can you think of any myths about advertising? What are they?

> **myth (n):** an idea that is not true but is believed by many people

3 Read the article, ignoring the gaps. Does it mention any myths you thought of? Does the author have a positive or negative view of the advertising industry?

 PREPARE FOR THE EXAM

Reading and Use of English Part 2

4 Read the first two paragraphs of the article. For questions 1–8, think of the word which best fits each gap. Use only one word in each gap.

 EXAM TIPS

- Remember to use only one word in each gap. Don't use contractions.
- Fill in the easy gaps first, then go back and try the harder ones.
- Read the text again when you have finished to check your answers.

Five myths about advertising

Advertising is the same as marketing.

No, it isn't! They're connected **(0)** _____ *but* _____ different. Marketing is about **(1)** _____ out what customers want and using that information to design and create products that meet their needs. Advertising is about trying to persuade people to buy your products once they have **(2)** _____ created. Advertisers don't make products, they sell them. So, working in advertising requires different skills **(3)** _____ working in marketing.

Anyone can learn to sell.

Absolutely not! It **(4)** _____ be true that training will help anyone to perform better in their work, but selling is a talent that you **(5)** _____ have or you don't have. It's **(6)** _____ of your personality. It's probably more accurate to say that someone who can sell, can sell anything – the skill is the same, **(7)** _____ the product. Training will make a good salesperson great, but it won't turn someone **(8)** _____ a salesperson who doesn't have selling in their soul.

It's a really exciting career.

It can be, yes. If you're part of the team that creates a really successful advertisement, it can be a lot of fun, and you'll get the sense of achievement that always results from doing something well. Just don't think it will be like that all the time. People in advertising work hard, they work long hours and they may not work at all if the product they're advertising doesn't sell. It's a tough industry to work in, there's a lot of competition and there's always someone who wants your job!

You'll make a fortune!

Well, you might, but it's never a good idea to go into a job thinking that it's an easy way to make money quickly. Think of the thousands of people working in advertising. Some of them will become extremely well-off, but most will not, as in any profession. You will need to be willing to work for a modest income while you're learning the job, perhaps for a number of years. With talent and perhaps a little luck, you may eventually earn a high salary.

Advertising is morally wrong.

There's nothing immoral or dishonest about advertising. The idea that selling is dishonest probably comes from the past, when sellers did not always tell the truth about the products they were selling. Today, advertising agencies must follow rules and there are severe penalties for any who do not. Advertising messages are often extremely sophisticated and may suggest that a product is better than it actually is, but it is illegal to make statements that are incorrect.

5 Answer the questions.

1 What is the main difference between advertising and marketing?

2 Does the writer think that it's possible for anyone to learn to sell? Why? / Why not?

3 Why is advertising a tough industry to work in?

4 What are the key features that might make you wealthy if you work in advertising?

5 Why are advertisers generally honest these days?

6 Match the **highlighted** words in the article to the meanings.

1 rich _____
2 difficult _____
3 not large _____
4 wrong _____
5 punishments _____

GRAMMAR Conditionals (1): review

1 Complete the sentences with the correct form of the verb in brackets.

1 If I _____ (hear) a noise in the night, I always get out of bed and check.
2 I feel tired if I _____ (watch) too much television.
3 You _____ (save) a lot of money tomorrow if you only buy things that are on offer.
4 Would you sponsor us if we _____ (form) a volleyball team?
5 Ice cream _____ (melt) if you leave it out of the freezer.
6 If I _____ (win) a lot of money, I'd buy a new house.
7 You _____ (have) an accident if you don't stop driving so fast.
8 I'd have slept better if I _____ (not play) on the Xbox until late.
9 If the government _____ (ban) advertising, they'd lose a lot of money.
10 If you had told me you were hungry, I _____ _____ (make) you a sandwich.

2 Rewrite the sentences using the third conditional.

0 We didn't know Dan was in hospital, so we didn't visit him.
If *we'd known Dan was in hospital, we'd have visited him.*
1 I loved the campaign, so I bought the product!
If _____
2 The skirt wasn't on offer so she didn't buy it.
If _____
3 I watched the film because I'd read a great review.
I wouldn't _____
4 You didn't ask me to sponsor you, so I didn't.
I would _____
5 She got the job because she asked all the right questions.
If _____
6 They didn't sell their products because they didn't advertise.
They would _____
7 I needed to go shopping, so I didn't go to the library.
If _____
8 We didn't meet you at the cinema because we didn't know you were going.
We would _____

3 Correct the mistakes in the sentences or put a tick (✓) by any you think are correct.

1 You can go to the beach if the weather will be good.
_____
2 I have a chance to prove myself, if you employ me.
_____
3 I would be very pleased if you came and visit me.
_____
4 Probably, if nothing would have happened, I would have lost anyway.
_____

VOCABULARY Adverb + adjective collocations

1 Complete the sentences with these adverbs.

actively	conveniently	environmentally
finely	naturally	nicely	ridiculously
well		

1 The hotel is _____ located within walking distance of the beach.
2 First, take the _____ chopped garlic and fry it gently in olive oil.
3 Please dispose of your rubbish in an _____ friendly way.
4 Tina is usually _____ dressed – so why does she look so untidy today?
5 I'm not a _____ talented singer, I'm afraid.
6 The weekend has a _____-balanced programme of activities.
7 Everyone passed the test because it was _____ easy!
8 My mother is _____ involved in a campaign to ban advertising to children.

2 Complete the second sentence using the correct form of the words in bold.

1 **Scientists** have **proved** that this method works.
This method has been _____.
2 It's **amazing** how **tasty** this fruit drink you made is!
This fruit drink you made is _____.
3 As an artist, he is **recognised** all over the **globe**.
He's a _____ artist.
4 We use only materials which are considered to be **safe** from an **ecological** point of view.
We use only _____ materials.
5 I'd love to be **independent** as far as my **finances** are concerned.
I'd love to be _____.
6 It's **incredible** how **economical** these electric cars are.
These cars are _____.
7 This information needs **updating** on a **regular** basis to be useful.
It needs to be _____.

1 Read the sentences in Exercise 3 quickly. What is Tom's talk about? ....

2 Look at each gap in the sentences in Exercise 3. What part of speech is needed to fill each one (noun, verb, adjective, adverb)?

✓ **PREPARE FOR THE EXAM**

Listening Part 2

3 You will hear a man called Tom Atkins talking about his summer working for an advertising agency. For questions 1–10, complete the sentences with a word or short phrase.

12

My summer job

1 Tom says it was his interest in .... which gave him the idea of a career in advertising.

2 Tom asked his .... to help him find work experience in an ad agency.

3 Tom thinks he got the job because his .... impressed the interviewer.

4 Tom uses the word .... to describe what he did with a long-term employee at the agency.

5 One of Tom's tasks was to make .... for clients who used the internet for publicity.

6 Tom found that .... were the least enjoyable part of the job for him.

7 Tom says that the .... at the agency was what most impressed him about working there.

8 The experience made Tom certain that he wanted to work in a .... in the future.

9 Tom stresses the importance of .... to anyone who wants a career in advertising.

10 Tom has a .... where people can follow what he is doing in the future.

4 Listen again and check your answers.

🔊
12

✓ **EXAM TIPS**
- This part of the exam tests your understanding of detail and specific information.
- The answers are all spoken in the recording, so you should write what you hear.
- You will hear the recording twice, so do not worry if you miss the answer the first time.

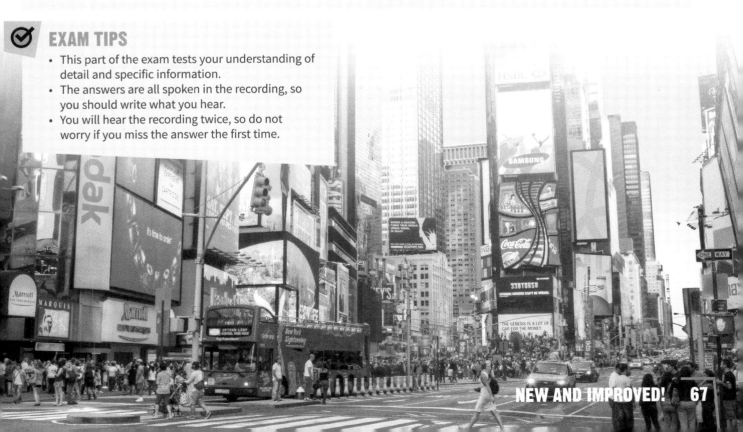

VOCABULARY   The media

1 Match the two halves of the phrases.

1	keep	**a**	about
2	keep	**b**	headlines
3	celebrate	**c**	up to date with
4	gossip	**d**	on current events
5	make	**e**	stories
6	make	**f**	you amused
7	comment	**g**	fun of
8	cover	**h**	achievements

1	3	5	7 ....
2	4	6	8 ....

2 Complete the advert with the phrases, or parts of the phrases, from Exercise 1.

CHILL OUT

Chill Out is a new internet magazine by students, for students. You'll find plenty to keep you ¹ _____ here – from the news that's ² _____ headlines in the national press, to our best student writers ³ _____ on current events around the university. Every week there's a new profile of a well-known ex-student, where we ⁴ _____ their achievements since they left. Our sports section will keep you up to ⁵ _____ with the latest results, and our 'Public Eye' page will give you all the ⁶ _____ about local celebrities. There are even cartoons which ⁷ _____ fun of public figures. You can be sure that we'll ⁸ _____ the stories that mean the most to you in your daily life on campus.

3 Complete the sentences so that they are true for you.

1 I keep up to date with the news by ....

2 The best bit of celebrity gossip I know is ....

3 A TV show that makes fun of politicians in my country is called ....

4 The thing that makes the headlines most often these days is ....

READING

1 What makes a good journalist? Write one important point, then read the whole article quickly to see if your point is included.

....
....
....

 PREPARE FOR THE EXAM

Reading and Use of English Part 3

2 For questions 1–8, read the first two paragraphs of the article. Use the word given in capitals to form a word that fits in the gap.

 EXAM TIPS

- Correct spelling is essential in this part of the exam, so always check yours.
- Remember that you may need to add a prefix, suffix, or both.

3 Now read the rest of the article and answer the questions. Choose from the four people, A–D.

1 Who recommends making stories as clear and short as possible? ....

2 Who mentions that joining the best team for you is crucial? ....

3 Who advises never to turn down any job offer? ....

4 Who emphasises the importance of telling the truth? ....

5 Who suggests working without pay initially? ....

6 Who says good writing can sometimes make the reader feel upset? ....

7 Who stresses the importance of factual accuracy? ....

8 Who recommends keeping up to date with current affairs? ....

JOURNALISM AS A CAREER

In spite of the rapid changes in the world of journalism, its (0) _POPULARITY_ (POPULAR) as a career choice remains high – which means that the (1) _____ (COMPETE) for jobs can be quite intense.

The (2) _____ (TRADITION) route into journalism used to be a job with a local newspaper, where you could learn the trade as a new recruit. But a sharp decline in advertising revenue has caused (3) _____ (FINANCE) trouble for small newspapers, and now very few can afford to take on (4) _____ (EXPERIENCED) staff who they have to train. Nowadays, the vast majority of (5) _____ (VACANT) are filled by graduates who have written for their university magazines or other publications, and have a large portfolio of work to show to a potential (6) _____ (EMPLOY). In other words, it is not easy to get started. But do not be (7) _____ (ENCOURAGE)! We have spoken to four established journalists who give you their top tips, not only for getting your first job, but also for making the most (8) _____ (EFFECT) use of your time there to help you become the best you can be.

A Zach
(writer for *The Chatterer*)

The most important thing I'm doing for my career is connecting with suitable people. Nothing in life is entirely about the individual, and if you don't find the right group to work with, you'll never be happy. I work with great people and even on terrible days, I'm better off than I would be if I had decided to compromise. To me, great journalism answers important questions people didn't even know they wanted answers to. It translates the emotions of a situation so accurately and deeply that the reader has no choice but to feel them as though he or she was there. It leaves the reader in a better or worse place than when he or she started, but never in the same place.

B Tina
(editor of *MaxRumours*)

If you want a career in journalism, say 'yes' to everything. Every job, however dull, gives you the chance to meet people. Don't worry too much about your first job – you need experience and it is important to remain open-minded, as in the future an employer will look less at the subject matter and more at your commitment to the task and your achievements. This is a hard industry to get into, and you need to take any opportunity that arises. Good journalism is about knowing the full details. The more you research your subject and find new ways to capture events and news, then the better your journalism will be. Triple check sources and tips, and make sure you're always 100% sure before you hit the 'submit' button.

C Nicky
(managing editor of victornewssource.com)

The number one thing I stress with new writers is that every single word in a sentence should be meaningful. Don't write complicated sentences around the facts when you can just come right out and say what you mean. Using fewer words is often more powerful, especially on the web. Identify the story and push it as far as it can go. Readers can sense when you're half-hearted or bored, and they'll forget about you if you don't write every story with passion. Good journalism is all about honesty, even if it means being honest about being wrong.

D Elizabeth
(freelance multimedia journalist)

Be informed: read news, watch news, and don't just limit yourself to the media you agree with. You will produce better work more quickly, ask more relevant questions and have better ideas if you are more aware. There's nothing more embarrassing than a journalist who hasn't bothered to get the facts together and doesn't know what they're talking about. The most important thing I did for my career was to get relevant voluntary work experience at the start. It doesn't matter what you do when you begin – on your CV it shows you were interested and determined enough to get yourself there.

I'm confident it was my unpaid job at the local newspaper that helped me get my first proper job in journalism and, as they say, the journey begins with that very first step.

---

4 **Match the highlighted words in the article to the meanings.**

1 related to what is useful or being talked about ....
2 agree to something which is not exactly what you want ....
3 extreme or very strong ....
4 significant, containing meaning ....
5 describe something successfully using words or pictures ....

1 Match the sentence halves.

1 If I hadn't bought that new laptop,
2 The performance would have been a disaster
3 I would have known what her problem was
4 If I had brought my swimming costume,
5 If I had spent more time studying,
6 Do you think you would have crashed the car
7 Would you be living in the United States now
8 If I hadn't eaten those prawns,

a if you were a more confident driver?
b if I was a doctor.
c I would be able to afford a holiday now.
d I wouldn't be feeling so ill now.
e if you weren't such a good actor.
f I might be at university now.
g if your father had taken that job with Microsoft?
h I would be lying by the pool right now.

1 .... 3 .... 5 .... 7 ....
2 .... 4 .... 6 .... 8 ....

2 Write mixed conditional sentences from the original sentences. Use *could* or *might* if you can.

0 I saw the film last week, so I know how it ends.
   If *I hadn't seen the film last week, I wouldn't know how it ends.*
1 He didn't bring his mobile phone. That's why he can't call for help.
   If ....
2 I don't have a degree, so I wasn't able to apply for the teaching job.
   I ....
3 Sandra doesn't enjoy horror films so she didn't come to the cinema with us.
   Sandra ....
4 We lost the match. That's why we're unhappy now.
   If ....
5 John never met the right person. That's probably why he isn't married now.
   John ....
6 I'm not good at cooking, so I didn't become a chef.
   If ....
7 They've got a new baby, so they didn't go on holiday in the summer.
   They ....
8 You broke the kitchen window. You haven't got any pocket money left.
   You ....

3 Correct the mistakes in the sentences or put a tick (✓) by any you think are correct.

1 If I hadn't got good grades at school, I don't study medicine now. ....
2 I think that our way of life would be very different if the telephone was not invented. ....
3 They told me that I could go on the school trip, if I had asked my parents first. ....
4 I'd have really liked to know what would have happened if you hadn't been there.
   ....
5 If the dog could speak, it would have told the old man the same thing. ....

1 Match the phrasal verbs to the meanings.

1 get across   ....
2 follow up   ....
3 bring up   ....
4 look into   ....
5 catch up on   ....
6 leave out   ....
7 back up   ....
8 clear up   ....

a introduce a particular subject
b deal with a (problem)
c make a person understand something
d investigate
e support
f take further action
g become up to date about something
h not include

2 Complete the sentences with the correct form of the phrasal verbs in Exercise 1.

1 We have a great politics teacher who is very good at .... ideas .... to us.
2 Did you ever manage to .... those problems you were having with the mobile phone company?
3 The journalist .... his review of the book with an interview with the author.
4 I was fortunate that my family .... me .... when I decided to change my college course.
5 I'm writing an article for the school magazine which .... the question of whether exams are getting easier every year.
6 I don't want to be .... of this meeting – why am I not on the list?
7 I don't read the news when I'm on holiday, but I always try to .... it when we get home.
8 You have .... some interesting points. Let's discuss them later.

A review

>> See *Prepare to write* box, Student's Book page 101.

1 **Read the exam task and answer the questions.**

1 What do you have to write a review about?
_____

2 Where will it appear? _____
3 Who will read it? _____
4 What information should you include in your review? _____

You see the following advert in a local magazine called *What's Going On*.

> **Film reviewers wanted!**
> *What's Going On* is looking for talented new film reviewers! Your task is to write a review of a film based around the news media. Tell us what the film was about, and describe its good and bad points. Would you recommend it to our readers?
> The best reviews will be published in this magazine.

Write your **review**.

2 **Read the film review quickly. Without putting the paragraphs in the correct order, can you tell if it is positive or negative?** _____

HEADLINE HUNTERS

A In general, I'd thoroughly recommend this
[1] **unusual** (_____) film to anyone with a sense of humour. If you like comedy, you'll love this classic.

B The idea for the film might not sound too exciting to you, but believe me, it's a [2] **very funny** (_____
_____) comedy that will make you laugh so hard it hurts. The script is fast-paced and [3] **amusing** (_____
_____), the lead actors are brilliant, and the music – a mix of indie pop and rap – really fits the film.

C A film I saw recently was **Headline Hunters**. It's set in a high school in the United States, and it's about the students who work on the school newspaper. The story focuses on two reporters who are always in competition with each other to write the best story. They are both
[4] **keen** (_____) to get the editor's job one day, and their attempts to impress become [5] **very silly** (_____
_____) as the film goes on.

D The only weak part of the film was the ending. I don't want to spoil it for you by saying exactly what happens, but I will say that it was a bit too 'Hollywood' for me. Why must they always have an emotional ending?

3 **Put the paragraphs in the correct order according to these general topics.**

Introducing the film _____
The positive parts _____
The negative parts _____
The conclusion _____

4 **Did the writer of the review answer all of the questions in the task?** _____

5 **Make the text more interesting by replacing the words in bold with these more descriptive expressions. (Write them in the brackets.)**

absolutely determined	highly original
quite witty	really hilarious	totally crazy

✓ PREPARE FOR THE EXAM

Writing Part 2 (A review)

6 **Write your own review in 140–190 words. Use the structure in Exercise 3 to guide you.**

✓ EXAM TIPS

- Answer all the points or questions in the task.
- Write about both the positive and negative aspects of what you are reviewing.
- Give your own overall opinion at the end, and a recommendation if appropriate.

VOCABULARY The world of work

1 Add vowels to complete the phrases about work.

1 b ___ dly p ___ ___ d
2 w ___ rk ___ ng l ___ ng h ___ ___ rs
3 m ___ k ___ ___ ___ l ___ v ___ ng
4 m ___ ___ t d ___ ___ dl ___ n ___ s
5 r ___ w ___ rd ___ ng
6 t ___ k ___ t ___ m ___ ___ ff
7 w ___ ll - p ___ ___ d
8 w ___ rk ___ ng sh ___ fts

2 Complete the sentences with the phrases in Exercise 1.

1 I don't get any time for hobbies because my job involves _____.
2 I don't care if I'm not rich, as long as I make _____, I'll be happy.
3 I'm quite good at getting things done on time, so a job where I have to _____ will be fine.
4 My job is really _____, so I can't afford any expensive holidays.
5 I don't get much money for my work, but I love it because it's so _____.
6 My father's used to _____ – one week he does 6.00 to 2.00, and the next week 2.00 to 10.00.
7 Not many jobs allow you to _____ _____ when you want, because they like you to be there!
8 I need a really _____ job because it costs a lot of money to live in this city.

3 Choose a phrase from Exercise 1 to describe either the person or the type of work they are looking for.

1 Suraya doesn't particularly want to earn a lot of money but she wants a job that she finds satisfying.

_____

2 Umit doesn't like work and has lots of hobbies.

_____

3 Anna is very flexible when it comes to working hours.

_____

4 Steve wants to buy a big house and drive a nice car.

_____

5 Carla doesn't like being at home and gets bored at the weekends.

_____

READING

 PREPARE FOR THE EXAM

Reading and Use of English Part 5

1 You are going to read an article about a young entrepreneur called Hannah. For questions 1–6, choose the answer (A, B, C or D) which you think fits best according to the text.

1 What do we learn about Hannah in the first paragraph?
   A She is influenced by her father.
   B She understands the importance of hard work.
   C She is willing to take chances.
   D She wishes her family was more ambitious.

2 When the author says Hannah 'was swindled' (line 19), this means she was
   A the victim of dishonesty.
   B taught how to do good deals.
   C angered by unfair treatment.
   D given poor advice by someone she trusted.

3 Hannah and her friend's bird-selling business failed because
   A people stopped wanting to buy pet birds.
   B they were charging too much for them.
   C the birds were difficult to keep.
   D they couldn't sell them quickly enough.

4 When Hannah worked at the chemist's shop, she revealed
   A an ability to cooperate.
   B a talent for marketing.
   C an interest in medicine.
   D a lack of respect for customers.

5 Regarding Hannah's attempts to make money, her parents
   A were happy that she was doing something she enjoyed.
   B didn't believe they would lead to academic success.
   C were proud of her achievements.
   D didn't take them very seriously.

6 What does 'it' refer to in line 61?
   A living with her parents
   B business ambition
   C formal education
   D publishing

 EXAM TIPS

• Always read the text before reading the questions.
• With 'incomplete sentence' questions, make sure you read **both** parts of the sentence in the question carefully.
• One question will usually ask you to deduce the meaning of a word or phrase. Read the text around the word or phrase to help you decide.

YOUNG ENTREPRENEUR

Hannah often wondered where she got her business sense from. It didn't come from her father, of that she was certain. When she was a child back in the 1980s, her dad was constantly in and out of work as a baker. Hannah couldn't understand why he hadn't realised that by baking and selling his *own* bread and cakes, instead of working long hours for someone else, he could make plenty of money of his own – much more than he was earning in the badly-paid jobs he kept getting. But he was a cautious man. Always making sure that nothing went so badly wrong that the family would have no money. Hannah, by contrast, was a risk taker – even at the age of eleven.

Hannah used to make extra pocket money by cleaning the cars of the few people who lived on her street. One day, while Hannah was finishing off her neighbour's Mercedes, the owner brought out a large box of old vinyl records. He said Hannah could take them, so she took them to the local second-hand record shop. This, it turned out, was the first time she
19 **was swindled**. The man in the shop looked at 11-year-old Hannah and said, 'These are mostly rubbish – I'll give you five pounds for all of them.' She was quite happy with that, as it was five times as much as she got paid for washing a car. But the next week her neighbour told her that the records were worth a great deal more than that. Hannah was furious, but it was a valuable lesson.

The next year she decided to start her own business. In partnership with her best friend Maria, they decided to start breeding budgies, a kind of small brightly-coloured bird. At the time, they were very popular pets among the kids at school, so it seemed like an obvious gap in the market. Indeed, once they got the pricing right, they sold quite a few. But they soon found that the budgies were multiplying faster than they could sell them. Eventually, Hannah's mum accidentally left the cage open and they all flew away. Hannah told herself that the market for pet budgies was declining anyway – it was just a passing fad.

At the age of 16, Hannah excelled at science, so she started doing a Saturday shift at a local chemist's to make some extra money. It wasn't very well paid, but she was enthusiastic, and introduced one of her ideas to the owner, Mr Pickles, and his staff. When a customer asked for a bottle of indigestion tablets, the staff were supposed to ask, 'Small or large?' – and most customers would say 'small'. Hannah suggested they say, 'Do you want the small bottle for two pounds or the extra value bottle for three pounds?' After that, nearly every customer chose the bigger bottle. Mr Pickles was very pleased, and gave her a raise.

With the money she saved working at the chemist's, Hannah bought a printer – they were quite expensive at the time – and started up a small business which she found much more personally rewarding: the student magazine. By this time, Hannah's parents were used to her little schemes. They weren't exactly encouraging, but they let her get on with things, provided her school work didn't suffer as a result. Her intelligence was obvious to them, and they expected her to carry on her education to university level and become a scientist of some kind. So it came as quite a blow when she announced that, after she completed her A-level exams, she was going to give
it all up and concentrate, alongside a new business *line 61* partner, on magazine publishing.

Little did they know that within a few years, Hannah would become one of the wealthiest young entrepreneurs in the country.

2 **Match the highlighted words in the article to the meanings.**

1 plans
2 an unexpected event that has a damaging or unpleasant effect
3 keeping animals for the purpose of producing young animals
4 happened in a particular and unexpected way
5 pain in your stomach after you have eaten something

GRAMMAR   Uses of verb + -ing

1 Correct the spelling of the -ing form where necessary.

1 I am *writting* to apply for a job in your company.
2 I keep *forgeting* to send you that photo from our holiday.
3 Do you admit *useing* the answer key when you do your homework?
4 *Running* is very good exercise.
5 He spends a lot of time *studing* in his bedroom.
6 What are you *planing* to do when you leave school?
7 Which TV documentary are you *referring* to?
8 My uncle, *beeing* a keen sportsman, is very fit.

2 Complete the sentences with the -ing form of the verbs in the box.

apply	arrive	do	feel	move
play	try	wait	watch	work

1 Stella's been _____ as a waitress in this café for most of the summer.
2 _____ for summer jobs is not my idea of fun, but I have to do it!
3 Dan spends a lot of time _____ on his Xbox when he should be studying.
4 Our football coach, _____ to get us to train harder, offered to buy us all burgers and chips if we won the match.
5 Why do you always insist on _____ ten minutes early for every class?
6 I don't really enjoy _____ reality TV shows, but everyone at school talks about them.
7 Jodie's mother is thinking of _____ to Canada to work as a translator.
8 I haven't been _____ very well recently, so I haven't done any work on the project.
9 _____ for the bus in the freezing cold, Jack decided it was time to get himself a new bike.
10 I don't mind _____ exercise in the gym, but I'd rather go out for a long walk by the river.

3 Complete the sentences about you. Use the -ing form of a verb.

1 Sometimes I dream about _____
2 I can't live without _____
3 I'm looking forward to _____
4 I don't enjoy _____
5 I've been _____ for years.
6 _____ makes me feel ill.

4 Correct the mistakes in the sentences or put a tick (✓) by any you think are correct.

1 I write this letter to say thank you for your hospitality. _____
2 Everyone panicked and started running towards the exit. _____
3 I don't mind to work hard and I feel good when I use my time efficiently. _____
4 I would prefer working with animals instead of helping in an office. _____

VOCABULARY   Word pairs

1 Make eight word pair phrases.

1 more   less
2 round   over
3 more   and   later
4 sooner   or   two
5 now   then
6 one   more
7 up   round
8 over   down

1 _____
2 _____
3 _____
4 _____
5 _____
6 _____
7 _____
8 _____

2 Choose word pairs from Exercise 1 to replace the bold words.

1 I enjoy going out for a meal **occasionally**.
_____
2 There are **approximately** 100 employees in this company.
_____
3 It's getting **increasingly** difficult to find a job these days.
_____
4 The temperature has been **rising and falling** all summer – I never know what to wear!
_____
5 Keep trying – I'm sure you'll find what you want **eventually**.
_____
6 We are having **a few** problems with the new system, but it's OK on the whole.
_____
7 We tried **repeatedly** to call you, but you never answered.
_____
8 I cycled **continuously in circles in** the park this afternoon, so now I'm exhausted!
_____

1 You will hear an interview with a young woman called Tina Jakes who is talking about the advertising business she started with a friend when she finished university. First, make notes on these questions.

1 What do you think she might enjoy about her work?

....

2 What are the most important qualities for a career in advertising?

....

....

2 Read questions 1–7 on the right. Underline the main idea in each question. The first one has been done for you.

3 Listen to the first part of the interview and choose the best answer (A, B or C) to question 1.

4 Look at this paragraph from the interview and underline the parts which gave you the answer.

> I didn't, really! It was Marcus's idea. I'd just graduated with a degree in psychology, and there aren't many opportunities available in that field. To be honest, I had a low opinion of the advertising industry at that time – you know: it's the business of lying to people to persuade them to buy things they don't need. But Marcus is a brilliant graphic designer, and he was looking for a partner in his new advertising business, so I thought – why not? Try it.

5 What parts of the extract above might lead you to the wrong answer?

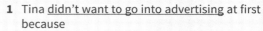

Listening Part 4

6 Listen to the complete interview. For questions 2–7, choose the best answer (A, B or C).

1 Tina <u>didn't want to go into advertising</u> at first because
   A she thought it was a dishonest business.
   B she wanted to be a psychologist.
   C she knew it was difficult to find a job.

2 What does Tina enjoy most about her work?
   A the opportunity to use her imagination
   B the personalities of the people she works with
   C the satisfaction of doing a good job

3 Tina does not enjoy her job when
   A she has to work on her own.
   B clients don't have a clear idea of their requirements.
   C there is a lot of pressure to complete a project on time.

4 How does she use a computer in her work?
   A to put together some initial ideas
   B to present a campaign to clients
   C to put the final touches to a campaign

5 Tina gets her ideas from
   A surfing the internet.
   B looking closely at a client's needs.
   C having meetings with her colleagues.

6 What does she look for in a new employee?
   A the ability to get on with others
   B a degree-level qualification
   C a wide variety of interests

7 When talking about her spare-time activity, Tina reveals
   A a desire to be a professional musician.
   B that she is very focused on her career.
   C a lack of concern for her personal finances.

7 Listen again and check your answers.

 EXAM TIPS
- Underline the main idea in each question and the key words in each option.
- The questions are in the order you will hear them, and are usually introduced by a question from the conversation.

VOCABULARY — Opinions and beliefs

1 Match the words and phrases to the meanings.

1 firmly believe in ....
2 there is no doubt ....
3 hard to deny ....
4 be convinced by ....
5 as far as X is concerned ....
6 bear in mind ....
7 go along with ....
8 keep an open mind ....
9 to my mind ....
10 be totally against ....
11 suspect ....
12 your view on ....

a be willing to consider new ideas or opinions
b be confident that something is good
c be persuaded by
d remember or consider something
e in my opinion
f it is certain
g in X's opinion
h think that something is probably true
i disagree entirely with
j your opinion of
k difficult to disprove / disagree with
l agree with

2 Complete the sentences with the words in Exercise 1.

1 He wasn't _____ by my arguments.
2 That, _____, is not a practical suggestion.
3 I hope his age _____ totally _____ him in the election.
4 What's _____ the government's youth policy?
5 We don't often agree, but I'd _____ you there!
6 There _____ that Simon has worked very hard on this project.
7 _____ concerned, you can do what you want.
8 I always try to _____ about new ideas.
9 It's _____ that this job is going to take longer than expected.
10 When I'm arguing with somebody, I always try to _____ that I might be wrong.
11 He _____ democracy, and I _____ that he always will.

3 Complete the sentences so that they are true for you.

1 I firmly believe in _____
2 I am totally against _____
3 I'm keeping an open mind about _____

READING

1 Read the title of the article and the first paragraph quickly. Where do you think the article is from?

a a textbook
b a newspaper
c a magazine

PREPARE FOR THE EXAM

Reading and Use of English Part 6

2 You are going to read an article about two systems of thought. Six sentences have been removed from the article. Choose from the sentences A–G the one which fits each gap (1–6). There is one extra sentence which you do not need to use.

A However, it is *system 2* which actually plays more of a secondary role in our lives.

B This phenomenon can also lead to the common mistaken idea that your successful decisions demonstrate your skill and talent.

C Every year businesses pay billions of dollars to try to answer these questions.

D In one study, volunteers were monitored with brain-scanning equipment.

E This has led some scientists to claim that we have no control over our own mind.

F It's a slow thought process that requires us to pay attention and concentrate.

G Nowadays, we still have the ability to react rapidly and naturally to situations.

EXAM TIPS

- Read the text and the sentences A–G for their general meaning.
- Look for links in the sentences before and after each gap in the text.
- Underline the important words and phrases in the sentences A–G and look for linking words.
- Read through the whole text with your answers in place to check it makes sense.

TWO SYSTEMS OF THOUGHT

How good are we at predicting what people will do – what magazine they will buy, what music they will download or what shoes they will choose for a party? **1 ☐** But we are still not very good at it. When it comes to human behaviour, the brain has been shown to have two different **approaches** to thinking. It doesn't matter how old you are or how confident you're feeling, it's all about what system your brain is using at the time.

The most common thought process is the automatic and fast approach which helps us to react quickly in dangerous situations. This is known as *system 1*, and dates back to the times of our prehistoric ancestors, who lived with a natural awareness of the dangers around them – bad weather, falling rocks and trees, and threatening animals. **2 ☐** Often it can feel like you're not thinking at all. Have you ever found yourself giving in to temptation and unable to say 'no' to buying that new jacket in the window? This is because *system 1* is in control – a human characteristic which the world of advertising tries to **exploit**!

System 2 is the opposite. **3 ☐** It kicks in when we're doing a complex mathematical sum, for example. This way of thinking helps us to make sensible **long-term** decisions like choosing which university to study at, or what type of car to buy. The problem is that *system 2* often starts to feel boring and so *system 1* takes over.

How often have you put down your homework or put off doing important jobs to go on social media or watch a TV soap?

We like to think that we go through life mainly using *system 2*. As individuals, we believe we are in control, always taking sensible and logical decisions. *System 1* type thoughts are reserved for special occasions when we can afford to relax a little – on holiday perhaps. **4 ☐** It behaves a bit like a supporting actor in a film who believes himself to be the **leading** character – but actually has little idea of what's going on!

Sometimes it's *system 1* that makes the right decision and *system 2* that gets it wrong. For example, professional sports teams put a lot of effort into a game plan, but often it's the unconscious human wish to do something differently that leads to a spectacular goal. **5 ☐** In actual fact, they are often just luck.

Perhaps one day scientists will be able to predict what decisions people will make by measuring neural activity. **6 ☐** They were asked to press either a left or a right button whenever they wanted. The researchers found they could predict which button the volunteers would press up to seven seconds before it happened – your brain seems to know what it will do before you do! Some scientists say our brains are just machines and we are not really in control of what's going on. Let's hope they're wrong! It's one thing to **be able to tell** which of two buttons a person will press, but I don't like the idea that science could one day tell me what decisions I will make in my life before I've even had the chance to make them!

3 Match the **highlighted** words in the article to the meanings.

1 know or recognise something from what you hear, see, etc. ....
2 ways of doing something ....
3 continuing a considerable time into the future ....
4 very important or most important ....
5 use or develop something to your advantage

GRAMMAR Subject–verb agreement

1 Complete the sentences with the correct form of the verb in brackets.

1 A number of people _____ (ask) me about the geography trip already.
2 The process for selecting students for the quiz teams _____ (be) now in place.
3 All of the students _____ (be) waiting in the hall.
4 Having more than three children per family _____ (contribute) to global over-population.
5 No one _____ (understand) how consciousness arose.
6 One of the scientists in the team _____ (be) only 20 years old.
7 The government _____ (plan) to increase funding for scientific research.
8 Politics _____ (be) not a very interesting subject for me.
9 Everyone in the class _____ (take) the English exam next week.
10 Both of Keira's sisters _____ (look) very much like her.

2 Choose the correct form of the verb. If both are possible, choose them both.

> ● ● ● ◄ ► 　　　　　　　 🔍 🏠
>
> Hi Alan
>
> I'm sorry to say that not much progress
> ¹ *has / have* been made in finding people
> to take part in our psychology experiment.
> Plenty of people ² *has / have* said it sounds
> interesting, but nobody ³ *has / have* offered
> to help yet, although a couple of my
> students ⁴ *is / are* thinking about it. I think
> taking part in an experiment ⁵ *frightens /*
> *frighten* them. Even my family ⁶ *isn't / aren't*
> keen, and I don't want to make them feel
> guilty, so I don't push them. I'm particularly
> disappointed that the science club ⁷ *hasn't /*
> *haven't* even replied to our request. I'll let
> you know if any more news ⁸ *arrives / arrive*
> tomorrow, but I'm not very hopeful.
>
> Best,
>
> Tina

3 Correct the mistakes in the sentences or put a tick (✓) by any you think are correct.

1 I don't think there is many athletics on TV today. _____
2 The food at both of the restaurant are different. _____
3 The atmosphere in both of them is informal, calm and friendly. _____
4 In some homes everybody have a computer.

VOCABULARY Plural nouns

1 Complete the puzzle, using the clues below.

1 the words of a song
2 the things a person owns
3 the place where someone or something is and the things that are in it
4 the outer area of a city or town
5 food and drinks
6 the list at the start of a book which tells you what the book contains
7 all the money you have kept for the future

Word down: _____

2 Complete the sentences with the words in Exercise 1.

1 We often go camping because we like to spend time in natural _____.
2 We will be serving _____ at two o'clock.
3 I would sing the song for you, but I've forgotten the _____.
4 Before I buy a book, I always read the _____ page.
5 My grandparents have a little house on the _____ of town.
6 Your _____ are all wet. Did it rain?
7 Please take all your _____ with you when you leave the train.
8 I spent all my _____ on a new bicycle.

WRITING | An essay (4)

>> See *Prepare to write* box, Student's Book page 111.

1 Complete the table with the linking words and phrases in bold, according to their function.

1 I don't often agree with my brother, **although** I respect his opinions.
2 Teenagers are not yet adults. **For this reason**, they shouldn't be allowed to vote.
3 I firmly believe in the value of education. **Consequently**, there is no doubt in my mind that it is worth paying for.
4 **In order that** we reduce crime, it is necessary to abolish poverty.
5 **Despite** having an open mind, I'm not convinced by your arguments.
6 **Since** not all politicians are trustworthy, we must have elections regularly.
7 There is no doubt in my mind about this. **Therefore** it is a waste of time trying to convince me I'm wrong.

Contrast	*although*
Purpose	
Reason	
Result	

2 Your English teacher has asked you to write an essay. Read the title and make some notes for each point.

> **'Some people say boys and girls should be educated in separate schools.'**
> **Do you agree?**
>
> Notes
> Write about:
>   1 relationships _____
>   2 discipline _____
>   3 (your own idea) _____
>   _____

3 Complete the essay with the linking words and phrases in Exercise 1. Use one of each function.

4 Read the essay title below and make some notes for each point.

> **'Some people say that parents put too much pressure on children to do well at school.'**
> **Do you agree?**
>
> Notes
> Write about:
>   1 importance of education _____
>   2 free time _____
>   3 (your own idea) _____

 PREPARE FOR THE EXAM

Writing Part 1

5 Write your answer to the question in 140–190 words. Use your notes and give reasons for your point of view.

 EXAM TIPS

- Take time to think and note down your ideas before writing the essay.
- Make a note of the vocabulary you want to use.
- Remember to use a logical structure for your essay.

In my country, nearly all schools have a mixture of boys and girls. ¹_____, the majority of the population has no experience of single-sex education. But separating boys and girls is quite common in other countries. So what are the advantages and disadvantages of each system?

It seems obvious that educating boys and girls in the same environment improves understanding between the sexes. This is important for adult life. In fact, it is essential ²_____ we can have happy and healthy relationships.

On the other hand, some people say that discipline is better in single-sex schools. ³_____, grades are higher and students are more successful in later life. In addition, both boys and girls might benefit educationally as they would not be distracted and would find it easier to concentrate in lessons.

As far as I'm concerned, it is hard to deny that single-sex education has some academic benefits for both boys and girls. ⁴_____ that, I am against it because the importance of understanding between the sexes is so great for the future happiness of everyone.

VOCABULARY Idioms

1 Match the two halves of the phrases to make idioms.

1	break	a	track of time
2	break	b	an eye for something
3	take	c	the ice
4	be	d	a pain
5	be	e	your mind
6	cross	f	someone's heart
7	have	g	your breath away
8	lose	h	a piece of cake

1 .... 3 .... 5 .... 7 ....
2 .... 4 .... 6 .... 8 ....

2 Complete the sentences with the correct form of the idioms in Exercise 1.

1 Oh, stop ....
– you're really annoying me!
2 That exam ....
– I'm sure I got 100%.
3 It never .... that we might not be able to get tickets for this concert. I'm so disappointed.
4 Do you know any good activities to .... when a new class begins?
5 I always take my aunt with me when I go shopping because she ....
a bargain!
6 It .... to see you so unhappy – is there anything I can do to help?
7 When we reached the top of the mountain, the amazing view ....
8 I'm sorry I'm late. I ....

3 Complete the second sentence so that it means the same as the first sentence, using the word given.

1 Watching my cat grow old made me sad. **HEART**
It ....
to watch my cat grow old.
2 Getting into the house through the back window was very easy. **CAKE**
It ....
to get into the house through the back window.
3 Have you ever thought about buying a bicycle? **CROSSED**
Has ....
to buy a bicycle?
4 When I first saw London from the air, the view really amazed me. **BREATH**
When I first saw London from the air, the view ....
....
5 Starting with a game is a good way to make everyone feel relaxed at a party. **ICE**
A good way ....
at a party is to start with a game.

READING

1 Read the title of the article and the first paragraph quickly. Ignore the gaps. Where do you think the article is from?

✓ **PREPARE FOR THE EXAM**

Reading and Use of English Part 3

2 For questions 1–8, read the first three paragraphs of the article. Use the word given in capitals to form a word that fits in the gap.

✓ **EXAM TIPS**

- Some of the answers will be plurals.
- At least one of the answers is likely to be a negative.

3 Choose the correct ending to each sentence.

1 According to the writer, Esperanto has *had varying success / been unfairly criticised / improved relations between countries*.
2 In the second paragraph 'foster conflict' means *make education difficult / interfere with politics / cause social problems*.
3 Esperanto is not officially taught in English schools because *it lacks cultural depth / very few people speak it / English is the international language*.
4 Supporters of Esperanto claim that *many famous people speak it / it has achieved a lot in a short time / soon everyone will understand it*.
5 Brian Barker says that *people need to be educated about Esperanto / the English language is unpopular / nobody speaks Esperanto*.

4 Match the highlighted words in the article to the meanings.

1 affecting or including a lot of places, people, etc. ....
2 people chosen by a group to represent them, especially at a meeting ....
3 questioned if something is true ....
4 when there's not enough of something ....
5 the fact of including many different things ....

ESPERANTO SPEAKERS LAUNCH A NEW DRIVE
TO GAIN INTERNATIONAL RECOGNITION

In a conference hall in Iceland tomorrow, (0) _CAMPAIGNERS_ (CAMPAIGN) from all over the world will gather to launch their latest attempt to get international (1) _____ (RECOGNISE) for the language they can all speak. The conference is held (2) _____ (ANNUAL), and the language they are promoting is Esperanto. (3) _____ (ATTEND) figures are expected to be around the 1,000 mark.

Esperanto has had an up-and-down history since it was created by Lazar Zamenhof in 1887 in (4) _____ (RESPOND) to linguistic divisions in his native Poland. He believed that language barriers foster conflict, and therefore set about promoting Esperanto as a 'neutral' second language that had no (5) _____ (POLITICS) history.

Nowadays, it is officially taught in around 600 primary and secondary schools around the world. However, attempts to get it officially accepted as a foreign language in English schools have so far been (6) _____ (SUCCESS). A spokeswoman for the Department of Education in the UK explained that the (7) _____ (DIFFICULT) in getting Esperanto taught as part of the national curriculum stems from the fact that there are no (8) _____ (LITERATURE) texts and no culture to interact with.

Supporters of the language argue that it is easy to learn and understand because it has a fairly simple grammatical structure. They point out that in its short history of over 130 years, Esperanto has established itself in the top 100 languages worldwide (out of a total of 6,800). It is also the 29th most used language on Wikipedia, ahead of Danish and Arabic. In addition, to argue against the UK government's point about the lack of literature, they say there is a 'rich body' of more than 50,000 titles which have either been translated into or written in Esperanto.

The delegates at the conference on Friday, who will be greeting each other with a cheerful _saluton_ (hello), would like to see it play a more important role in the workings of institutions like the UN and the European Union. 'There are two urban myths about the international language problem,' said Brian Barker of the Esperanto Society. 'One is that everyone speaks English, and the other is that no one speaks Esperanto. Both are untrue and both need to be challenged.'

The language has not been without heavyweight supporters. Actors, businesspeople, scientists, artists and novelists – the breadth of Esperanto's appeal cannot be underestimated. Millionaire financier George Soros and _Star Trek_ actor William Shatner (who even starred in a movie filmed entirely in Esperanto) have promoted it, and others who have spoken the language include J.R.R. Tolkien and Leo Tolstoy.

There is no shortage of campaigners ready to promote the language, therefore, although whether it will become more widespread in the future remains to be seen.

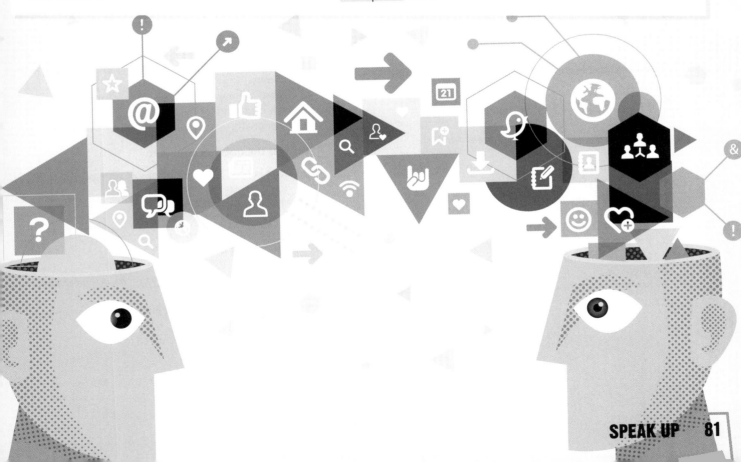

1 Complete the sentences with *a*, *an*, *the* or – (no article).

1 We haven't been to _____ theatre in Park Street for _____ ages.
2 'What did you have for _____ breakfast?' 'I ate _____ eggs that were in _____ fridge.'
3 I learned to speak _____ French when I was _____ engineering student in Paris.
4 Unfortunately, _____ film was _____ disaster, and we left _____ cinema halfway through.
5 Do you have _____ explanation for _____ terrible mess in this room?
6 Why is she speaking with _____ foreign accent? I thought she was _____ native English speaker.
7 _____ best thing about this book is that it makes _____ really nice coffee mat.
8 London is _____ great city to live in if you like _____ noise and _____ traffic.

2 Choose the correct words.

1 *Much / Plenty of* people around the world speak Esperanto.
2 We've had *a few / a bit of* difficulty collecting all the data.
3 There is a small *number / amount* of students who haven't finished their project.
4 I'm sorry, I don't have *many / some* tickets left.
5 This job is going to take a large *number / amount* of effort for very *little / few* reward.
6 I don't want *a lot of / many* food tonight, thanks – I'm going training.
7 *Any / Several* of our members have expressed an interest in the trip.
8 Tara has *plenty / a few* questions she would like to ask you.
9 I can give you a hand quickly, but I really haven't got *some / a lot of* time.
10 *Little / Some* native American languages are still spoken in North America.

3 Complete the sentences with *(a) little* or *(a) few*.

1 I tried, but it was _____ use.
2 I'm worried about my sister, who has _____ friends.
3 Eventually, _____ diners entered the restaurant.
4 This soup needs _____ salt and pepper.
5 Surprisingly, _____ children in the school could spell correctly.
6 Please be quick. We have _____ time to waste.
7 I've got _____ time now, if you want to talk about the homework.
8 There were _____ students at the lecture – not the whole group, but enough.

4 Correct the mistakes in the sentences or put a tick (✓) by any you think are correct.

1 I hope you will have a great fun. _____
2 Can you imagine the school where you can study only the subjects you enjoy? _____
3 Furthermore, I am a very reliable and responsible person. _____
4 However, not much people like to read a book. _____
5 I was really happy to spend few days with you. _____

1 Choose the correct answer.

1 I love trains – they are my favourite _____ of transport.
   A means   B journey   C way
2 Excuse me. Do you know the _____ to the airport?
   A means   B journey   C way
3 The best _____ to learn something is to practise it.
   A means   B journey   C way
4 Is there a slight _____ that you might come and visit us this month?
   A opportunity   B possibility   C happening
5 That was a very _____ film. I couldn't stop laughing!
   A funny   B sad   C fun
6 Did you get the _____ to talk to the director about your ideas?
   A opportunity   B possibility   C happening
7 We went to the park, but it wasn't much _____.
   A funny   B happy   C fun
8 I _____ my leg during a football match.
   A harmed   B injured   C damaged
9 Be careful you don't _____ my camera.
   A harm   B injure   C damage
10 Don't worry, the snake isn't poisonous – it won't _____ you.
   A harm   B injure   C damage
11 Can you _____ how much money I have in my pocket?
   A know   B observe   C guess
12 I learned how to play chess by _____ my dad play with his friend.
   A knowing   B observing   C guessing

2 Answer the questions for you.

1 What is your favourite means of transport?

2 What do you find funny?

3 Do you usually know all the answers to the exercises, or do you guess some?

4 What is the longest journey you have ever made?

5 Have you ever missed an important opportunity?

6 Have you ever injured yourself?

LISTENING

1 Look at the questions on the right. Underline the main points in each question.

2 You will hear people talking in eight different situations. Listen to the first extract and answer question 1. Choose the best answer (A, B or C).

3 Look at the extract and underline the part which gave you the answer.

Girl: So, what did you think of your first rugby match? Impressed?

Boy: It was a bit confusing, actually. I still don't understand the rules.

Girl: So you didn't enjoy it? That's a shame.

Boy: Oh, I wouldn't have missed it for the world! I just lost track of what was going on, that's all. But the players are obviously very good at what they do.

Girl: So, would you come again?

Boy: Yes, but I'll be sure to eat before we go next time. I was starving for most of the game.

Girl: Sorry – it didn't cross my mind that you'd be hungry! Next time we'll have lunch at the clubhouse restaurant. It's very good.

4 Listen to all of the extracts and match them to the photos (A–H).

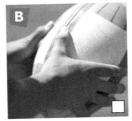

Listening Part 1

5 Listen to the complete task. You will hear people talking in eight different situations. For questions 1–8, choose the best answer (A, B or C). Then listen and check your answers.

1 You hear two people talking about a rugby match they've just seen.
How does the boy feel about it?
A happy to have experienced it
B unimpressed by the skills of the players
C pleased with the quality of the food available

2 You hear two friends talking about a new gym.
What do they both think about it?
A It is a bit too crowded.
B It is rather expensive.
C It is well designed.

3 You hear a girl talking about a jacket she bought online.
What is she complaining about?
A The jacket was the wrong size.
B She was charged too much.
C The jacket was delivered too late.

4 You hear a dancer talking about his life and work.
What is he trying to explain?
A why his mother was so successful
B his reasons for becoming a dancer
C the similarities between classical and modern dance

5 You hear two friends talking about going on holiday.
Why is the girl worried about going on holiday?
A She might lose her role in the school play.
B She won't be able to afford to pay for anything.
C She thinks her absence will badly affect the school play.

6 You hear an interview with a young businessman.
What is his business?
A hiring out motorcycles
B repairing motorcycles
C selling advertising space

7 You overhear a boy telling a friend about an Esperanto class he attended.
How is he feeling?
A discouraged by the teacher's methods
B uncertain about whether or not to return
C optimistic about making progress

8 You hear a review of a TV documentary which is based on a book.
What does the reviewer think about the documentary?
A It is disappointing.
B It is better than the book.
C It contains too much information.

 EXAM TIPS

- Read the question carefully before you listen.
- If you are still not sure of the answer after one listening, underline the key words in the question before you listen again.
- Use the second listening to reject the options which you think are wrong.

Acknowledgements

The authors and publishers acknowledge the following sources of copyright material and are grateful for the permissions granted. While every effort has been made, it has not always been possible to identify the sources of all the material used, or to trace all copyright holders. If any omissions are brought to our notice, we will be happy to include the appropriate acknowledgements on reprinting and in the next update to the digital edition, as applicable.

Key: U = Unit.

Text
U1: Adapted text from 'Read it!', previously published in *AQUILA magazine*, March 2013: https://www.aquila.co.uk. All rights reserved, New Leaf Publishing 2012-2014. Reproduced with permission; **U3:** Adapted text from 'Experience: I've been to the quietest place on Earth' by George Mickleson Foy, *The Guardian* 18/5/2012. Copyright Guardian News & Media Limited 2012; **U5:** Adapted text from 'Colosseum'. Adapted with permission from *Encyclopaedia Britannica*. Copyright © 2019 by Encyclopaedia Britannica, Inc; **U6:** Adapted text from 'Read it!', previously published in *AQUILA magazine*, March 2013: https://www.aquila.co.uk. All rights reserved, New Leaf Publishing 2012-2014. Reproduced with permission; **U12:** Adapted text from' Spreading the Love: Juan Mann' by Jenna Good, *WHO Magazine* 30/1/2008. Reproduced with permission from WHO Magazine and Jenna Good; **U14:** Adapted text from 'Defining Ecotourism', by Michael Merg at www.untamedpath.com. Reproduced with permission; **U15:** Adapted text from 'Charities losing out thanks to social media 'slacktivism'', Metro 11/11/2013. Copyright Associated Newspapers Limited. Reproduced with permission; **U20:** Adapted text from 'Ĉu vi parolas Esperanton? Esperanto speakers launch new drive to gain international recognition' by Richard Garner, *the Independent* 25/7/2013. Copyright © Independent. Reproduced with permission.

Photography
The following photographs have been sourced from Getty Images.

U1: georgeclerk/iStock Unreleased; Azenith Umipig/EyeEm; **U2:** Rasica/iStock/Getty Images Plus; © Marco Bottigelli/Moment; oneinchpunch/iStock/Getty Images Plus; **U3:** Anup Shah/ DigitalVision; Vertigo3d/E+; **U4:** ERIC CABANIS/AFP; Johner Images; Assembly/Photodisc; FatCamera/iStock/Getty Images Plus; Celia Sanchez/Image Source; Oliver Rossi/Corbis/Getty Images Plus; GrapeImages/E+; **U5:** SOPA Images/LightRocket; Dinodia Photos/Hulton Archive; retroimages/DigitalVision Vectors; Lingxiao Xie/Moment; kali9/E+; **U6:** Caroline Purser/DigitalVision; **U7:** FatCamera/E+; irina88w/iStock/Getty Images Plus; **U8:** James Darell/Cultura; Comstock/Stockbyte; Tetra Images; Zave Smith/Image Source; Pierre-Yves Babelon/Moment; **U9:** Echo/Juice Images; **U10:** vm/E+; e_rasmus/E+; **U11:** Cultura RM Exclusive/Nancy Honey; David Merron/500px Prime; Barry Winiker/Photolibrary/Getty Images Plus; laflor/E+; **U12:** Dani Abramowicz/FilmMagic; monkeybusinessimages/iStock/Getty Images Plus; asiseeit/E+; **U13:** Gregory Costanzo/The Image Bank/Getty Images Plus; PeopleImages/E+; DGLimages/iStock/ Getty Images Plus; Ismailciydem/iStock/Getty Images Plus; ajr_images/iStock/Getty Images Plus; Caiaimage/Robert Daly/ OJO+; Andersen Ross Photography Inc./DigitalVision; **U14:** jez_bennett/iStock/Getty Images Plus; Pierre-Yves Babelon/ Moment; photography by Kate Hiscock/Moment; **U15:** Caiaimage/ Sam Edwards; adamkaz/E+; **U16:** Tashi-Delek/E+; OlegAlbinsky/ iStock Unreleased; **U17:** Maskot; Yuri_Arcurs/E+; Leland Bobbe/ Image Source; PeopleImages/E+; izusek/iStock/Getty Images Plus; **U18:** monkeybusinessimages/iStock/Getty Images Plus; Westend61; **U19:** Steve Debenport/E+; dszc/iStock/Getty Images Plus; Westend61; SteveStone/E+; **U20:** Orion Publishing; Caiaimage/Chris Ryan; PeopleImages/iStock/Getty Images Plus; BJI/Blue Jean Images; Carol Yepes/Moment; krblokhin/iStock Editorial/Getty Images Plus; blueskyline/iStock/Getty Images Plus; Kenneth Canning/E+; Jon Ortega/EyeEm.

The following photographs have been sourced from other library/ sources.

U1: Penelope Lively 2011/HarperCollins; Little, Brown UK; Zdenko Basic (illustration)/Mandy Norman (design); Troubador Publishing.

Front cover photography by MirageC/Moment/Getty Images.

Illustration
Rory Walker; Dave Smith (Beehive Illustration Agency).

URLs
The publisher has made every effort to ensure that the URLs for external websites referred to in this book are correct and active at the time of printing. However, the publisher takes no responsibility for the websites and can make no guarantees that sites will remain live or that their content is or will remain appropriate.

The publishers are grateful to the following contributors: cover design and design concept: restless; typesetting: emc design Ltd; audio recordings: produced by Leon Chambers and recorded at The SoundHouse Studios, London; project management: Carol Goodwright